C000042554

LIFE AFTER
BRISTOL CITY

The Author

Mark Leesdad has been a Bristol soccer fan since 16 December 1961 when, aged thirteen, he was cajoled into taking his cousin Kevin to see City play Notts County at Ashton Gate. From that day on he was hooked. 'We won 6-0; the line-up was Cook, Briggs, Thresher, Etheridge, Connor, Casey, Rogers, Atyeo, Tait, Williams and Derrick – and "Big" John scored four and Alex Tait got two,' he recalled. 'Thanks Kev.'

Later on, Mark found his niche in writing, spending a number of years with the public relations offices of two major companies, dealing with the media, writing press releases and acting as editor of their in-house magazines. These days Mark, who has two sons and two granddaughters, writes a weekly 'Memory Lane' column (plus a number of match reports) in the local paper with the best Sunday sports pages in the south west, *The Sunday Independent*.

LIFE AFTER
BRISTOL CITY

MARK LEESDAD

This book is dedicated to the memory of my sister Linda Thompsett.

First published 2007

STADIA is an imprint of
Tempus Publishing Limited
The Mill, Brimscombe Port,
Stroud, Gloucestershire, GL5 2QG
www.tempus-publishing.com

© Mark Leesdad, 2007

The right of Mark Leesdad to be identified as the Author
of this work has been asserted in accordance with the
Copyrights, Designs and Patents Act 1988.

Modern photography © Phil McCheyne, 2007

All rights reserved. No part of this book may be reprinted
or reproduced or utilised in any form or by any electronic,
mechanical or other means, now known or hereafter invented,
including photocopying and recording, or in any information
storage or retrieval system, without the permission in writing
from the Publishers.

British Library Cataloguing in Publication Data.
A catalogue record for this book is available from the British Library.

ISBN 978 0 7524 4154 2

Typesetting and origination by Tempus Publishing Limited.
Printed in Great Britain.

Contents

Acknowledgements

I've always felt that you could get bogged down with 'thank yous'. To me, there's nothing worse than watching an award show when the grateful recipient of an award goes on and on, thanking everyone from the midwife who delivered them to the local milkman. That said there are certain people that I must thank.

To begin with, my old office manager Eric Bradford, who inadvertently got me into the writing game, and to two of my old bosses, Christine Foster and Bill Edwardes, who encouraged and supported me – huge 'thank yous'. Also, thanks to another ex-boss, Richard Smith, who dragged me kicking and screaming away from my carrier pigeons and typewriter, and forced me to learn to use a computer (badly).

Good photography is vital to the success of any publication. I am indebted to a photographer that I have worked with for many years – Phil McCheyne of Nailsea – who has worked with me on this project, taking practically all of the modern-day photographs featured in this book. Phil also does weddings, bar mitzvahs, christenings, passport photographs, retirements…!

As far as the playing days pictures are concerned, I am grateful to the many players who loaned me photographs taken from their scrapbooks, photograph albums and, in some cases, cardboard boxes and suitcases stored in their attics. Also, many thanks to Bristol Rovers historian Mike Jay, and the various newspapers who helped out. Throughout, we have endeavoured to ensure non-breach of copyright and have not knowingly used photographs that bore copyright stamps.

I must also thank Tempus Publishing for showing faith in me and this project.

And of course, to probably the most important of all, my eternal and grateful thanks to our subjects. Those players of yesteryear who gave up their time to welcome me into their homes or places of work in order to make this book possible and to tell me their reminiscences – some of which are not included! – about their playing days.

Finally, yes I have gone on a bit and I'm sure to have left somebody important out, my thanks to you for buying this book. I'd like to think it's one of the finest things 'what I have ever writ' and if you get half as much pleasure reading it as I did researching and writing it, I'm a very happy man.

Mark Leesdad

Far left: Author Mark Leesdad.

Left: Photographer Phil McCheyne.

Introduction

Tinker, tailor, soldier, sailor, rich man, poor man, beggar man, thief. When I was a kid, if we had prunes and custard for 'afters', you always counted the prune stones against each of the occupations in the old tinker tailor rhyme, to see what your future career would be. If only life were that simple.

But what about our heroes on the soccer field? And not just the long-serving headline heroes. For some would-be stars, their soccer careers were nearly over before they'd even begun. What were they destined to become once their professional playing days were over?

In *Life After Bristol City*, I've not only looked at their footballing careers, but also their lives after soccer. Many of them, quite wisely, had learnt a trade either before their footballing days as professionals had kicked off, or before they had ended. Many had obviously sought inspiration from popular songs. Brian Drysdale, for example, could well have been influenced by 'If I were a Carpenter', while John Galley may have been inspired by The Beatles 'Baby You Can Drive My Car'. And number one in the list of inspirational tunes would have to be 'Please Mister Postman'.

Some people say that nostalgia isn't what it used to be, but I'm not so sure. If, like me, you love to look back, particularly in relation to your Ashton Gate heroes, and find out what happened to them when they hung up their boots, then this book is for you, or perhaps a friend, relative or loved one.

VIC BARNEY (Senior)

There probably aren't too many former City players who have also played football at the highest level in Italy. Vic Barney senior (more about that 'senior' tag later) has done just that, having played soccer for Reading, Bristol City, Grimsby and Italian giants Napoli.

Vic's footballing ability came to the attention of the Italian team towards the end of the Second World War. An infantryman, Vic was stationed in Naples in 1945 and turned out a number of times for the army representative side. A talented inside forward who had represented his county, he was offered the chance to play for the Napoli team. 'I was a lone Englishman in an Italian club side – it was a wonderful experience,' said Vic.

At the end of his army days, Vic bade farewell to his Italian teammates and returned home:

> I wanted a career in football, so I got on the train from Oxford, where my family lived, and went to Reading and asked for a trial. Anyway, I had to come back a few days later and ten minutes later was called off the pitch. I thought that was that, but to my delight, they'd seen enough of me to ask me to play in a forthcoming reserve game.

Vic's reserve game went well and he was duly signed up, lining up in the next first-team match. 'We played Crystal Palace and won 10-2, a record win for Reading, and I got a couple of goals, so that wasn't a bad start,' chuckled Vic. 'The next game we only scored seven!'

Vic went on to enjoy over two years with The Royals before being sold to Bristol City, 'Bob Hewison was the manager who brought me to the club and he was very good to me,' said Vic. Thirty-one senior games and five goals later, though, Vic was on his way. 'There was a boardroom takeover and Bob left the club. I wasn't happy with that and didn't want to stay anymore, so I asked for a transfer.'

Next port of call was Grimsby Town, where bonuses took on a different form than at most clubs. 'The average wage was around £8 a week, with a £2 bonus for a win and a £1 for a draw. Because the directors at Grimsby were all trawlermen, we also used to get boxes of fresh fish left at the dressing room door!'

Vic was to have one season at Grimsby – 'a great club, I was sorry to leave them' – before he headed back to the Oxford area to captain Headington United, later to become Oxford United.

Sadly, Vic died a few months after this interview. He was immensely proud of the fact that his two sons also made an impression in the game. Duncan turned out for Oxford City, while Vic Barney junior played at Bristol Rovers.

Training with Bristol City in 1949.

A more recent picture of Vic, in a Napoli shirt
he was presented with and a signed football.

LEN BOND

The name's Bond – Len Bond 001. Stirred not shaken. Mission? To stop the enemy getting through.

This particular Bond, Len not James, signed schoolboy forms for Bristol City in 1967 and became an apprentice in 1969:

> I was doing well in goal for the youth team, but ruptured a kidney in training and missed out on playing Leeds in a quarter-final Youth Cup match. Ironically, that's how Ray Cashley, who'd been playing full-back, took over in goal and went on to make over 260 senior games as City's keeper.

After coming back from injury, Len made his senior debut for The Robins in the last game of the 1970/71 season – a 2-2 draw at Blackburn. He made another two senior appearances the following season, before being loaned out to Exeter City. 'I was originally due to spend a month at Exeter, but stayed for six,' recalled Len. The following year he played in 13 games for Bristol City, before hitting the loan trail again. 'I had a month at Cardiff, a month at Colchester, then Torquay and finally Scunthorpe,' explained Len. 'By the time I was eighteen I'd already played over fifty League games.'

In 1973/74 Len got to put on City's senior goalkeeper's shirt 20 times, but over the next three seasons, he added just two more appearances. On the plus side, Len did get to spend time in the States, when he was loaned out to the St Louis Soccer Stars. 'I spent five months there and loved every minute,' said Len with a smile.

Back home, the chance of first-team football with a move to Brentford saw Len depart for Griffin Park. 'I had three years there, played over 150 games and won their Player of the Year award twice,' said Len.

A change of manager meant a change of fortune for Len. 'Me and the new manager didn't really see eye to eye, so I moved on,' he explained. Len had the choice of going to top club Chelsea or Exeter City. No choice, you might think. 'Chelsea were very honest and explained that they wanted me as cover, while Exeter were offering first-team football, so I went there,' Len told me.

'Brian Godfrey, a very good manager, was boss at Exeter and I had three happy years there,' said Len. Such was his respect for Godfrey that he followed him to non-League Weymouth.

After Weymouth Len moved to Bath City, but, with a newsagents in Exeter to run, found the travelling too much and moved on to the side he used to support as a youngster, Yeovil Town: 'That was a fantastic move for me.' A spell at Gloucester City, where he was managed for the third time by Brian Godfrey, followed, before Len moved into coaching:

> I got a call from Exeter, asking me to be the club's goalkeeping coach, so I took my coaching badges and jumped at the chance. Then, out of the blue, Gary Johnson, then manager at Yeovil, got in touch, asking if I fancied moving in the same role at Yeovil – and that's where I am today.

In addition to his role as goalkeeping coach at Yeovil, Len runs his own sportswear company – Len Bond.com – supplying kit and equipment to teams, schools, colleges and universities all over the country. He lives in Taunton with his partner Marilyn.

Len in his goalkeeping days at City.

Today Len runs his own
sportswear company.

JACK BOXLEY

Jack Boxley is such a nice bloke that you could never imagine him 'being sent to Coventry', but he was. Coventry City that is, when Bristol City transferred him to the Midlands club!

Prior to his move to Highfield Road, Jack had been a crowd favourite on the left wing at Bristol City. He signed for The Robins in 1950, having been spotted playing for Birmingham non-League side Stourbridge. 'Villa, Wolves and Fulham were interested in signing me, but City manager Pat Beesley offered me first-team football, which was good enough for me,' Jack pointed out.

That was in August 1950, with City paying £2,000 – a sizeable fee for a non-League player in those days – and the promise of sending their first team to Stourbridge for a friendly match. A dead-ball specialist – penalties, free-kicks and corners were food and drink to Jack – his prime objective was to supply the ammunition for strikers Arnold Rodgers and John Atyeo with his pin-point centres. And supply the ammunition he certainly could, playing a major role in the City side which won the Third Division (South) championship at the end of the 1954/55 season. 'We had a very good side and scored over 100 goals,' said Jack.

As well as striking up a good relationship on the field with 'Big' John (Atyeo) the two were good friends off the field, each acting as the other's best man.

In December 1956, Coventry City paid £5,000 to take Jack and teammate Jimmy Rogers to Highfield Road. 'It was handy Coventry signing the two of us, as we'd travel up together for matches and so on,' said Jack.

Their partnership for The Sky Blues lasted two years, with Rogers returning to Ashton Gate in 1958, before Jack also made the return trip to Bristol City in 1960, although Jack proudly points out that before he left, he was part of the Coventry side that won promotion from the newly formed Fourth Division. 'To get promotion once in your playing career is nice, but to get it twice is fantastic.'

On his return to Bristol City, Jack went on to complete 213 senior appearances for The Robins, scoring 35 goals, before calling it a day.

Life after tearing down the wing for City saw Jack take up a new career as a car salesman at nearby Winterstoke Garages. He went on to give them the same sterling service and more – some thirty-five years altogether – that he'd given as a player just down the road at Ashton Gate. Now retired, Jack lives in Long Ashton with his wife Patricia. They have a son, a daughter and five grandchildren.

Winger Jack Boxley in his playing days

A driving force even today.

WAYNE BRAY

'We didn't have a lot of choice in the matter – we had to cope and we had to learn fast.' That's the verdict of Wayne Bray, one of the young players thrust into City's first team, following the departure of the 'Ashton Gate Eight'. 'There were players like myself, Rob Newman, Jon Economou and Mark Smith, suddenly pushed into the senior side, we had to sink or swim, it was as simple as that,' added Wayne.

A member of the successful Bristol boys' team, Wayne also picked up seven caps for England Schoolboys, scoring for them at Wembley. He joined City as an apprentice in 1981 and three months later found himself making his first-team debut in a 0-0 home draw with Fulham. That same month he got the first of his two senior goals in a 3-1 win at Preston North End:

> The funny thing was that the manager had given me a rollicking at half-time for shooting from distance. Anyway, five minutes into the second period, I caught the ball just right and let fly with a thirty-yard screamer which flew past their keeper Martin Hodge and into the net.

Wayne's only other goal came in a home match with arch rivals Rovers:

> That wasn't a bad effort either – another effort from about thirty yards which curled into the net. And to do it against 'the old enemy' Rovers, and at the East End, now that was a bit special. When I joined the club, Bobby Houghton was in charge. Then I played under Roy Hodgson and after he was sacked, Gerry Sharpe had a spell as caretaker manager and didn't do bad, losing just one of his six games in the manager's chair. Then came Terry Cooper.

The vastly experienced Terry Cooper, who had played for the club in the late 1970s and had managed Bristol Rovers for a while, was charged with stabilising the team, now in the Fourth Division. It soon became apparent that Wayne was not part of Cooper's plans, and after just ten appearances that season he was released.

After leaving City, Wayne played non-League football at Weymouth, Weston-super-Mare, Bath City, Bristol Manor Farm and Dundry.

Away from football, Wayne is a partner in a kitchen fitting business. Married to Julie, the couple live in the Brislington area of Bristol and have three young children, Josh, Kate and Chelsea.

Right: Wayne in action for City.

Below: Wayne today, finishing off another kitchen installation.

DAVE BRUTON

Former defender Dave Bruton can always expect 'a welcome in the hillsides' when he crosses the bridge to Wales, having served first Swansea and then Newport County with distinction, after kicking off his career with Bristol City.

'I had some very good seasons with The Swans, winning promotion three times,' recalled Gloucester-born Dave, a 6ft-plus former central defender. 'Then I had four years at Newport County, winning promotion, the Welsh Cup, and getting to the quarter-finals of the European Cup-Winners' Cup.'

Dave crossed the bridge in 1973, but prior to that looked to have a long and promising career in the red and white of Bristol City. He was a member of the successful 1969 City youth team that enjoyed a good run in the Youth Cup competition, finally going out to a Spurs side that included the likes of Graham Sourness and Steve Perryman. 'There were some very good players in our youth team and I think seven or eight of us went on to make the first team,' Dave pointed out.

Signing for City as an apprentice in the summer of 1971, Dave got his first-team call-up the following November, in an away match at Sunderland. 'I was up against big Dave Watson, who alternated between centre half and centre forward,' said Dave. 'We did OK, getting a 1-1 draw at Roker Park.'

Under the management of Alan Dicks and John Sillett, things looked bright for the young centre half. 'I owe John Sillett a lot, he was an excellent coach,' said Dave, who went on to make a dozen appearances that season.

The following year, though, Dave was still fighting to claim a first-team place. 'The trouble was that City had five or six central defenders at the time and I only made a handful of games that following season.'

In August 1973, a £30,000 bid from Swansea manager Harry Gregg saw Dave and colleague Danny Bartley head for The Vetch. When Gregg departed, his successor started something of a revolution. 'John Toshack – he really got the club going on a roller coaster,' recalled Dave with a smile. A mix of existing players, plus former Liverpool stars brought in by 'Tosh', saw the club rise from Fourth to Third and then to Second Division.

With his first-team chances starting to be reduced as Toshack brought in more players, Dave was happy to move down the road to Newport County. Manager Len Ashurst obviously valued Dave's dedication and leadership skills, making him team captain. The side went on to win promotion out of the Fourth Division, and won the Welsh Cup, 'Those were certainly heady days for County,' agreed Dave. But, at thirty-one, a persistent knee injury saw Dave quit full-time football.

Winding down his playing career, Dave had spells at Gloucester City, Forest Green and Trowbridge, plus a season as player-manager with Cwmbran Town in the Welsh League. For some years Dave has worked in finance and insurance. Married to Maxine, the couple live in the Thornbury area of Bristol and have two teenage children, Sophie and Adrian.

Right: Dave Bruton in his playing days.

Below: Checking his road map before setting off on his patch, Dave Bruton today.

TERRY BUSH

One of the most dedicated and honest professionals to put on a Bristol City shirt, that's Norfolk-born Terry Bush. He notched up 166 starts in City's red and white between 1960 and 1970, scoring 45 goals in the process.

Never one to continually grab the headlines, an honest and dedicated player, Terry was happy to let the other players take the spotlight during his career. But, when the chips were down, you knew he would give 110 per cent, whether playing at centre forward or, towards the end of his career, wing half.

Terry joined the Bristol City ground staff as a sixteen-year-old in 1959. He remembers the first time he pulled on a City shirt in earnest – a reserve match against Chelsea at Stamford Bridge:

> Not a bad place to start eh? There were some useful lads in that Chelsea reserve side as well… Peter Bonetti, Terry Venables, Bobby Tambling… Peter Doherty was my first manager at City. He was very keen on developing youngsters, which was very good for a lot of us young ones. Then came Fred Ford, a great manager and a great guy. After Fred had departed, in came Alan Dicks, who I would have to say was technically the best.

Over the years Terry had tussles with some of the toughest centre halves around, but had no hesitation in naming his hardest opponent. 'George Curtis at Coventry,' he replied straight away, when asked. And the best player he's played with? 'Oh there were plenty of very good players, but Bobby Kellard sticks in my mind.'

The end of the 1969/70 season saw Terry bid farewell to City. But not for him the merry-go-round of playing out his days at other clubs. He left the professional game and joined the Transport and General Workers Union, where he gained as much respect for his commitment, enthusiasm and honesty as he did from fellow soccer professionals. 'I suppose you could say I was a negotiator, acting at tribunals for workers who had been unfairly dismissed – that sort of thing.'

The loyalty he had shown to Bristol City was equally evident with the TGWU and he spent the next thirty years with the organisation before he retired.

At the time of our photo call, Terry was on crutches, having undergone a third hip operation. 'I had the first hip replacement a couple of years ago, but the second operation didn't go so well and I had to go back in again,' he said.

Married to Ann for over forty years, the couple have a son and daughter and also have a grandson.

Right: Terry Bush in action.

Below: Recuperating from his third hip operation.

RICKY CHANDLER

When Ricky Chandler joined City as an apprentice in 1978, he couldn't have had any idea of what was in store. 'Alan Dicks was the manager then and the club was playing in the top flight,' Ricky pointed out. By the time Ricky made his senior debut, coming on as a substitute in January 1981, the club was already in freefall, having lost their First Division status. He went on to play in the last seven games of that season, as the team suffered a second successive relegation season:

> I'd played a couple of games before the financial crisis hit the club, but once all the experienced pros had agreed to leave (the 'Ashton Gate Eight'), it was only the younger, inexperienced players who were left. We were just kids, without any 'old hands' in the side to help us. We certainly took some punishment from the more experienced pros in the opposing sides.

And the toughest defender that Ricky has had to face? 'Mickey Droy of Chelsea – a mountain of a man.'

Back in the Third Division (now Coca-Cola League One) Ricky played 34 games, scoring eight goals, his first senior strike coming in a 2-1 defeat at Plymouth Argyle. But, with the club having lost their senior players out of financial necessity, relegation to the bottom division was inevitable.

Terry Cooper was the man at the helm, as the club set about stabilising. The end of the 1982/83 season saw them finish in fourteenth position, with Ricky playing nearly 30 games and scoring another eight goals.

Despite this return, the club let Ricky go and he moved on to spend a couple of seasons at Bath City and then Yeovil Town (still a non-League club at the time), managed by former Bristol City star Gerry Gow. Three seasons at Brian Godfrey's Gloucester City followed, before Ricky finished his playing days at Weston-super-Mare.

After leaving professional football, Ricky went into the sports equipment business. He spent a year with Puma, moved on to Hi-Tec and for the past three years has been with the Swindon-based STAG (Sports Traders Alliance Group) where he is a director. 'The business has been going really well and we have 320 retail outlets to supply up and down the country,' he said. 'In fact, business has gone so well that we have had to move to bigger premises earlier this year.'

On the domestic front, Ricky lives in the Headley Park area of Bristol with wife Rachel, teenage son Joe, who is a promising sweeper with Oldland Juniors, and young daughter Emily.

Ricky in his City playing days.

Ricky Chandler today.

PAUL CHEESLEY

You could understand it if former Bristol City star Paul Cheesley felt bitter about the way life has treated him. These days though, the only time the word 'bitter' ever really crosses his mind is when he has to change a barrel of best bitter at his public house The Knowle Hotel in the Broadwalk area of Bristol.

A natural centre forward, not afraid to go in where it hurts, Paul's front-line leadership played a major role in helping The Robins win promotion to the top flight. At that time he had also been called up by Don Revie for the England Under-23 squad, and although League commitments had seen him cry off, it was fully expected that he would be selected again. And, in City's first match in the First Division (now the Premiership), he scored the winner over Arsenal in a 1-0 win at Highbury.

Life was certainly sweet then for the highly-rated striker. Enter the cruel hand of fate. Just three days after the Arsenal win, Paul went up for a high ball with Stoke City's international goalkeeper Peter Shilton, twisted his knee as he landed, and, despite brave attempts at a comeback, that was the end of Paul's professional soccer career.

Although born just a few miles from Ashton Gate, Paul arrived at City via Norwich. That was in December 1973, with manager Alan Dicks paying £30,000 for the lad from Easton-in-Gordano. Paul made his Robins debut in Second Division match against Leyton Orient on New Year's Day, scoring his first goal for them in April against Carlisle. Between then and the end of the 1974/75 season, he clocked up 24 appearances (plus three as sub) and scored four goals.

But it was in the historic promotion season (1975/76) that Paul came into his own, missing just four League games. His 15 goals, just three behind top scorer Tom Ritchie, saw City finishing as runners-up to Sunderland to gain promotion to the 'promised land' of Division One.

Then, just two games into the season came Paul's injury and with it the loss of one of the best centre forwards to don a City shirt. He was a player seemingly destined to enjoy top flight and international success, with or without City. 'I was just very unlucky,' says Paul philosophically. 'It was a complete accident.'

After leaving soccer Paul worked as a rep for a while, before going into the licensed bar trade. After a spell running The Star at Twickenham, he and his wife Debbie now run The Knowle Hotel, just a couple of miles from the City ground. And Paul has certainly not severed his ties with the club. He is president of the City Supporters' Trust and has been match-day host on many occasions.

Right: Paul Cheesley as a very young striker.

Below: 'Cheers' – Paul behind the bar.

BRIAN CLARK

Following in dad's footsteps, that was former City star Brian Clark. He netted nearly a century of goals for City, as well as consistently finding the net for the clubs he went on to play for.

These days Brian lives in the Whitchurch area of Cardiff:

> I'd finished my League career in Wales, my daughters went to school there and my wife's job was there, so it made sense to live there. On top of that, we really love the area and I got a job with a local firm when I finished playing.

A member of the Bristol boys' team that won the English Schools Trophy, Brian joined Bristol City in 1960, following in the footsteps of his dad Don Clark, who played 136 games before retiring in 1951. During his City career Clark senior netted 82 goals. Son Brian bettered that with 89, plus another 133 on his travels.

Brian made his debut for The Robins at the end of the 1960/61 season – a 3-0 win over Brentford. The following season he made eight senior appearances and by the start of the 1962/63 season he was a permanent fixture in the side, forming a deadly partnership with 'Big' John Atyeo and 'Shadow' Williams. The trio continued to flourish throughout the following season and by the end of the 1964/65 season, City were on the verge of promotion to the Second Division. It was Brian who got the all-important first goal in the 2-0 win over Oldham that clinched promotion in the final game of the season.

The amiable striker continued to find the net in City's first season in the higher grade and, when Atyeo retired at the end of that season, it was assumed that Brian would be 'Big' John's long-term successor. Sadly it was not to be. A loss of form, something every striker goes through at some stage in their career, saw Brian depart the following year, leaving for Huddersfield Town.

The move to Huddersfield brought Brian another 11 goals from his 38 outings, before what turned out to be a dream move to Cardiff City, with Brian forming a deadly partnership with John Toshack. He went on to enjoy 185 games for the Welsh side, finding the net 75 times. 'I think scoring the winner against Real Madrid in the European Cup-Winners' Cup is the one I enjoyed the most,' he said.

After five years at Cardiff, Brian was off again. The next stop was Bournemouth – 12 goals and 30 games – and then Millwall, where he enjoyed 71 first-team games, netting 16 times. The chance to go back to his adopted home was too good to turn down and Brian returned to Cardiff in the 1975/76 season. His League career concluded with two seasons 'down the road' at Newport County, before calling it a day at the end of the 1978/79 season.

'I joined a Cardiff-based company which specialised in supplying protective clothing in South Wales and the South West and I used to visit councils and industrial customers as a health and safety representative,' said Brian. After sixteen years he moved to take a similar position with a rival company in Swansea, before retiring.

A Cardiff resident for thirty years, Brian lives with wife Gillian. They have two daughters, Allison and Jacqueline, and a baby granddaughter, Emily.

Above: A typical Brian Clark goal, as he finds the net against Portsmouth.

Right: Back at Ashton Gate.

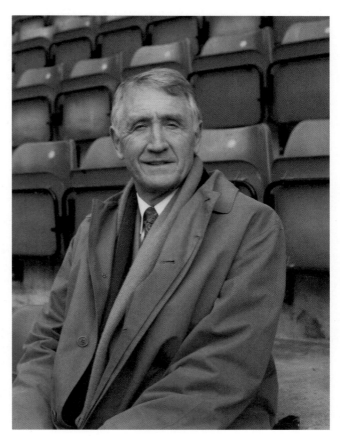

JANTZEN DERRICK

One of the most gifted and talented players to ever run out at Ashton Gate – that was Jantzen Derrick. And if Jantzen could have combined those natural talents with consistency, there can be no doubt that he would have gone on to a bigger and better stage for his skills.

A key member of the England Schoolboys team, Jantzen was quickly snapped up by City. He made the first of his 292 starts on the left wing against Lincoln City in 1959, aged just sixteen. His obvious skill shone through, and before he had reached his eighteenth birthday, he was a first-team regular.

Playing out on the right or left wing, he could dazzle one week, turning defenders inside out and setting up the likes of 'Big' John Atyeo, while the following match, he could be almost anonymous.

One of Jantzen's biggest supporters was the then City manager Fred Ford, who knew that on his day, Jantzen could turn on the magic and be a match-winner. But when Fred made way for Alan Dicks in 1967, the writing was on the wall. Dicks began to rebuild the side he wanted and it soon became clear that his rebuilding plans didn't include the skilful but inconsistent winger. He made his last appearance for City in a home match against Middlesbrough on 16 January 1971 – the game in which Gerry Sharpe's career ended with a badly broken leg.

When Jantzen packed his bags and left Ashton Gate, it wasn't to sign for another club in the Football League. The chance to play in France for the famous Paris St Germain, where his silky skills would be more appreciated, was much too good a chance to be missed. 'Going to France, living in Paris and playing for such a great club was a wonderful opportunity and one not to be missed,' summed up Jantzen.

After a season in France, Jantzen returned home, stepping down from the professional ranks. After leaving full-time soccer, most of Jantzen's time has been spent in a career selling commercial vehicles. 'Don't ask me why I got into this line of work, but I do enjoy it,' he said. 'It's certainly a different world from playing soccer.'

Still living just a goal-kick away from the ground, Jantzen is usually one of the first to put his name down when the club have an old boys' reunion.

Above: Jantzen in action for City in the 1960s.

Right: Busy at work, Jantzen Derrick today.

ALAN DICKS

Despite the fact that he never actually played for The Robins, it would be wrong not to include in this book the man who probably achieved more for Bristol City than anybody else – former manager Alan Dicks:

> Promotion to the old First Division – now that was something special for everyone associated with the club. When I first came to Ashton Gate they were involved in a relegation battle (from the old Second Division) so just keeping them up in the first few seasons was an achievement in itself.

But despite spending a great deal of time facing 'the drop', City enjoyed a fair bit of cup success:

> We did have some good cup games; Leeds and Spurs stand out as teams we played well against. Promotion, of course, was very, very special, as was the draw at Coventry at the end of our first season in the top flight, when a draw kept both clubs up.

On the subject of Coventry, it was there that Alan cut his coaching teeth, when Jimmy Hill was turning the club around. 'I joined Jimmy as his assistant manager and coach,' said Alan. 'Jimmy was smashing – a single-minded man who knew what he wanted. He did a fantastic job there.'

Of course, Alan had 'played a bit' himself. He started off with Dulwich Hamlet, played for Millwall reserves and then signed for Chelsea, being a member of the squad that won the championship in 1955. After eight years at Stamford Bridge, Alan spent three years with Southend United, before joining the Jimmy Hill revolution at Coventry.

Keen to make the step up from assistant manager, Alan took the City job and breezed into Ashton Gate with a whole wealth of ideas and tactics that he learnt from his time at Coventry. He also had an eye for bringing good players to Ashton, with fans' favourites John Galley and Norman Hunter two of his most popular signings.

In 1980, after thirteen years at the helm, and with the team spiralling down the divisions and going into financial meltdown, Alan was relieved of his duties. After a short period working for a sports promotional company, Alan took his management skills overseas, managing teams in Athens, Cyprus and America. He also had a spell in charge of Fulham.

Now retired, Alan's domestic life has been as eventful as his soccer career. The holder of both British and American passports, Alan has been married four times – wife number four being his first wife Moira. They live in the Henleaze area of Bristol and have five children and eight grandchildren.

> I was very lucky. Managers today simply don't get enough time. I was given the time by the City board to develop a successful side and I shall always be grateful for that.

Watching from the sidelines during his time as a manager Stateside.

'Definitely a reluctant gardener – my wife will know this shot was stage-managed!'

DICKIE DOWN

It's a fair bet that whenever a new manager comes into a club he'll want to change the personnel, from the coaches to the players. And, if new players are brought in that he thinks will strengthen the side, it follows that some of the ones he's inherited will be moving on. So it was with Dickie Down.

Dickie joined Bristol City as an apprentice in 1965 and made his debut for the club when he was seventeen. A highly-rated local centre forward, the future looked bright at Ashton for the young striker. 'My first game was at Coventry and I didn't even know I was playing until the morning of the match,' recalled Dickie. 'I was marked by George Curtis who was known as "The Iron Man" – what a baptism!'

Dickie went on to make a handful of appearances, scoring five goals in the process and it was looking good for him, until a spin of the management merry-go-round. 'Manager Fred Ford obviously rated me, giving me an early chance in the first team. In fact, I'm sure he did rate me because he signed me on again later in my career,' Dickie pointed out. Sadly for Dickie, Fred fell victim to the management axe and new boss Alan Dicks decided on changes. 'Dicks didn't rate me, which was his prerogative, and told me they'd accepted a bid from Bradford Park Avenue, so I was on my way. With hindsight I should have dug my heels in and stayed put,' said Dickie.

Looking back, Dickie acknowledges that going to Bradford Park Avenue, then in the old Fourth Division, was not a good move. 'I had eighteen months there and soon realised it was a big mistake,' he stated. On the plus side, though, Dickie at least had the company of former City teammates Chuck Drury and Graham Tanner, who also made the move to Park Avenue.

After over thirty games at Bradford, Dickie moved on to Second Division side Oldham Athletic. 'I enjoyed my time at Boundary Park, playing more than forty games for them,' said Dickie.

A chance to move back home was on the cards when Bristol Rovers made a move for him:

> I very nearly signed for them, but got a call from Fred Ford advising me to leave it for a few days. Fred then became manager at Swindon and offered me a contract, and knowing that Fred wanted me clinched it for me, and I signed for them instead.

Dickie went on to play two seasons at The County Ground, before dropping out of League football. 'I was struggling a bit with injuries and a ruptured Achilles tendon spelt the end of my playing days,' explained Dickie.

Out of football, Dickie held a variety of jobs, mostly driving, but his footballing injuries even put paid to a working career outside of soccer. 'I had some good times, notably at City, where there were a great bunch of lads, and some not so good times, but that's life,' summed up Dickie, who lives in Fishponds with his wife Lin.

Dickie Down in action for City.

A recent return to Ashton Gate for the former striker.

BRIAN DRYSDALE

Former Bristol City full-back Brian Drysdale, or 'Chippy' or 'Speedy' to his friends, always knew that when his playing days were over, he'd have a trade to fall back on. 'I started out at Lincoln City in 1959. The money wasn't particularly good, but the club insisted that their players learn another trade just in case they didn't make the grade,' explained Brian.

For a while it seemed that Brian would need to fall back on that second career. Between 1959 and 1965 he made just 21 League appearances for The Imps. A transfer to the League's perennial strugglers Hartlepools United didn't seem to be the answer, until a certain Brian Clough began to turn things around in his own unique management way. 'He was certainly a one-off and must have rated me, because he put me straight in the side,' said Brian.

Consistent displays at left-back for The Pools – he went to make 170 senior appearances for them – soon had the scouts flocking to the Victoria Ground. Bristol City's bid of £10,000 saw Brian packing his bags in 1969, and heading south to Ashton Gate, replacing the long-serving Alec Briggs in the no.3 shirt.

For the next three seasons Brian was an ever-present in the side. What he lacked in height – Brian was 5ft 7ins in his stockinged feet – he made up for with his tenacious tackling, his ability to overlap down the left wing and his pin-point crosses. He went on to make nearly 300 senior appearances for The Robins and was a member of the side that finally won promotion to the top flight. Not renowned for his goalscoring, Brian still chuckles at the memory of one of his three League goals – a forty-yarder against Bolton Wanderers that had more to do with a very strong wind than his shooting skills!

Having played a major role in getting City into the First Division, Brian's place in the team came under threat as the side struggled against the country's finest. The signing of Norman Hunter and the subsequent repositioning of captain Geoff Merrick to left-back meant it was time for Brian to start looking elsewhere for first-team football. He went on to spend a season on loan at Reading, followed by a year at Oxford United, where a broken leg was to spell the end for his Football League career.

After seeing out his footballing days at Shepton Mallet and Frome Town, Brian called it a day and went in search of his carpentry tools. He still keeps himself very fit and turns out in charity matches whenever the call comes. 'It's nice to see the lads again when we get together for matches,' he said.

On the domestic front, Brian lives in Stockwood with his daughter Mandy and son-in-law Nick. Sadly, his wife Linda died about eleven years ago. He's also got a son, Jason, who enjoyed football success with Watford, Newcastle United and Swindon Town.

A rare picture of Brian (centre) having a shot in the opposition's penalty area.

If I were a carpenter – Brian Drysdale at work.

JACKIE DZIEKNOWSKI

The phrase 'fans' favourite' or 'soccer legend' is often overused when talking about footballers, but there's no doubt amongst City supporters that one of the most popular and skilful players to ever don the red and white shirt was Polish international Jackie Dzieknowski.

Born in Warsaw in 1962, Jackie had been a success with Scottish giants Celtic, who had paid a transfer fee of around half a million pounds to bring him from Polish League football to Celtic Park in 1989. Already established in the international side (he made his debut for them at the age of nineteen), he went on to make nearly half a century of League appearances for The Bhoys, scoring ten goals:

> Glasgow supporters are very passionate about their football and there is big rivalry between Celtic and Rangers. I enjoyed playing for Celtic, they had a very good side and the derbies and also the European Cup games were good for me.

A mixture of surprise and delight was the general reaction when City's (then) manager Jimmy Lumsden persuaded Jackie to come to Bristol, paying the Scottish giants a £255,000 transfer fee. He soon showed he was worth every penny, scoring on his debut against Southend and then stealing the show when City dumped Leicester City (then in the top flight) out of the FA Cup at snow-covered Filbert Street.

Another Jackie 'highlight' came in a home match with Wolves a couple of months later, when he scored both goals in a 2-0 win, despite having had thirteen stitches in a leg injury. 'That was a very happy day,' said Jackie, with a smile.

When Lumsden left Ashton Gate, his successor Dennis Smith not only recognised Jackie's value to the team, he also brought in the perfect foil to partner him up front, Andy Cole. The pair were a perfect match, enhancing each other's skills and strong points – Jackie, with his ability to take on defenders and create space, and Cole for his knack of finding the net. 'We played well together,' summed up the likeable Pole.

Sadly, it wasn't to last. Cole was sold to Newcastle for a handsome profit and former teammate Russell Osman, who took on the role of player-manager, decided that the more workmanlike side he wanted to build couldn't afford the luxury of Jackie's individualism – a decision that upset many City supporters.

'After I left City, I agreed not to sign for a rival English club, so I left for home,' said Jackie. He returned to former club Legia Warsaw and also had a year and a half with FC Cologne in Germany.

These days, Jackie (his actual Christian name is Dariusz, but no one calls him that) lives in his native Poland. Having won 63 caps for his country, he is now the coach for the national Under-19 side.

Jackie (centre) pictured in his City days, with former teammates Andy Llewellyn (left) and Andy Cole.

Jackie out sightseeing on a return trip to Bristol.

ALEC EISENTRAGER

It seems hard to believe, but it if hadn't been for the dark days of the Second World War, a certain Alois 'Alec' Eisentrager would almost certainly never have been seen in the red and white of Bristol City. But, having been taken prisoner of war and transported to England, he went on to make over 200 appearances for The Robins.

'I was called up to the Luftwaffe at the age of sixteen in 1943 and the following year was captured on the Belgian-Dutch border,' explained Alec (nobody ever called him Alois). Having been taken prisoner, Alec saw out the rest of the war at a number of POW camps in Britain, where his footballing skills soon became apparent. 'We spent a lot of that time playing football against local non-League sides,' he explained. 'After the war I thought I'd stay for a year or so and signed for Trowbridge Town', he added.

A dazzling inside forward or winger, Alec was spotted by Bristol City and was happy to become a pro. Not that the wages were anything like those for today's players. 'We were on £12 a week in the season and £10 in the summer, less £1 9s 0d rent for the house supplied by City,' he chuckled. In those far-off days practically every professional football club had a number of 'club houses' for their players to live in.

It was in 1949 that Alec signed on the dotted line and he soon became a crowd favourite, particularly when doing the occasional bicycle kick – something very new to the game then. That same year he even hit the net four times in one match, with Newport County on the receiving end of his match-winning skills at Ashton Gate. 'We had some great players in those days – Arnie Rodgers, Tony Cook, Dennis Roberts, Ernie Peacock, who was my best man and, the greatest of them all, John Atyeo,' he said.

Between 1949 and 1958 Alec went on to make a total of 240 senior appearances for City, scoring 47 goals, before going back to non-League action, playing for Merthyr Tydfil. After working in the printing and stationery trade he went on to join Cam Gears, a local engineering company. The company had a useful soccer team and it wasn't long before Alec was persuaded to manage the side.

Now just over eighty years young, Alec is retired from working life and lives with his wife Olwyn, not far from the seafront at Clevedon. They have two daughters and two sons.

Alec in action in the 1950s.

Looking back through his soccer scrapbook,
Alec today.

KEITH FEAR

Former Bristol City star Keith Fear is senior salesman for Bristol Fruit Sales at the Wholesale Fruit Centre in Bristol's Albert Crescent. There is only one word to describe his job: hectic, very hectic. Fielding calls from two mobile telephones and a landline, Keith is kept busy dealing with deliveries, collections and ensuring that his customers – wholesale fruit suppliers – get exactly what they want in a very time-orientated business:

> I've worked here in 'the market' for about fourteen years or so. I get up very early (his alarm clock is set for 3.20a.m.!) and from the minute I arrive it's non-stop. Quite often there are wagons waiting to load up and supply their customers – schools, restaurants, pubs, hospitals – long before we are open.

But enough for now of oranges and apples, let's go back to Keith's football roots. He signed professional forms for City in 1970. Between then and the 1976/77 season, he clocked up 169 senior appearances, scoring 35 goals. A talented midfield player, he could dazzle supporters and opponents alike with his silky skills, but like many such players, on a bad day he could be anonymous. However, in Keith's time, the good days outweighed the bad.

No City supporter from that era can (or wants to) easily forget the two FA Cup matches with the mighty Leeds United. This was 1974 and the men from Elland Road were one of the top teams in the country. City were given little chance on paper, but an inch-perfect lob by Keith over the Leeds keeper gave City a highly creditable 1-1 draw at Ashton Gate. Now, if City had been given little chance of success for the first match, they were given no chance at all for the replay at Elland Road. But fairy tales do sometimes come true, and it was an inch-perfect pass from Keith that gave his colleague (and now one of his customers) Donnie Gillies the chance to score the only goal of the game.

Inconsistency and tactical team selections meant that Keith was never an automatic choice, and a cartilage operation created a further setback. Keith spent four months playing for St Louis Soccer Stars in America in order to regain fitness. 'That was a very enjoyable experience. I was getting paid to have a holiday and get fit and I got the chance to play against the likes of Pele and George Best,' he pointed out.

After returning home, Keith had loan spells with Hereford United and Blackburn Rovers, before being transferred to Plymouth Argyle. In his two seasons there he clocked up 45 appearances and spent an eight-match loan spell with Brentford, before winding up his League career at Chester.

Looking back, Keith is quick to praise his former City boss Alan Dicks: 'We didn't always see eye to eye, but he's the best manager I've played under and the best manager Bristol City ever had.'

Away from the hustle and bustle of the fruit centre, Keith lives at Pensford with his wife Valarie. He has a son and daughter from his first marriage (sadly his first wife Lynda died) and a stepson.

Above: Keith (right) during his playing days at City.

Right: Another busy day at the fruit centre.

JOHN GALLEY

When centre forward John Galley arrived at Ashton Gate in December 1967, he was the perfect Christmas present for the club and the fans, going on to notch up nearly 200 senior appearances and just nine goals short of a ton. As the fans used to sing (with apologies to Al Johnson): 'We'd walk a million miles for one of your goals, John Galley.'

Not surprisingly, there were a few eyebrows raised when John limped, quite literally, into Ashton Gate to sign for the club. Alan Dicks had splashed out £25,000 to bring the centre forward to the club from Rotherham United. The only trouble was, John was suffering from tendonitis and had his foot in plaster. John was clearly not fit and the City board nearly had a fit when they found out the striker they'd sanctioned the money for was on crutches.

But Dicks' faith in the 6ft target man was justified when he scored a hat-trick on his debut a few weeks later. And it was John who went on to repay the manager's faith with a sackfull of goals that kept City in the Second Division and Alan Dicks in a job.

Born in Derbyshire in 1944, John's first professional club was Wolverhampton Wanderers in 1962. After just five senior appearances, and two goals, he was transferred to Rotherham United, where he soon began attracting the scouts with his goalscoring exploits – netting 48 times in 112 games. On his arrival at City, he struck up a deadly partnership with Chris Garland and scored 18 times in 28 games. A virtual ever-present the following year, his goal tally rose by another 22.

And so it went on, with John averaging a goal every two games. But, after 195 games and 91 goals, the fans were dismayed when, in December, 1972 their terrace favourite was sold to Second Division rivals Nottingham Forest for £33,000. It was the turn of Forest fans to get a Christmas present. But John was never able to quite recapture his goalscoring feats with Forest. There was a short spell on loan at Peterborough, before he switched clubs – and position (to centre half) – with a move to Hereford United.

John still got 10 goals for United in 80 appearances and was a member of the team there which won promotion. 'It was quite ironic in a nice sort of way,' added John. 'We won the old Third Division championship the same season that City went up to the top flight.'

With his playing days winding down, John had a season with non-League side Telford, before finishing off with a spell at Atherstone in the Southern League. 'After I finished football I learnt to be a printer,' John told me. 'Then I became a rep selling paper to printers in and around the East Midlands.'

These days John runs his own executive taxi business in Nottingham, where he lives with his wife Elizabeth. The couple have a son, daughter and young grandson.

John Galley watches for a mistake by the Birmingham keeper while playing for City in 1971.

John Galley today.

CHRIS GARLAND

With the retirement of legendary City star John Atyeo, the Ashton faithful were looking for a new local hero. They wouldn't have to wait long. Having avidly watched 'Big' John tear opposition defences apart, the young Chris Garland was determined to follow in his hero's footsteps.

'John Atyeo was "Mister Bristol City" – a legend – an unbelievable player,' summed up Chris. A skilful forward, Chris signed as an apprentice for City in May 1966 and made his debut in a 2-0 home win over Preston the following November. Sadly, he never got to play alongside 'Big' John, Atyeo having retired from the game as Chris was signing on.

Chris scored his first senior goal in September 1967 and went on to make 33 full appearances, scoring nine goals. By the turn of the year he had been joined up front by John Galley and the 'G force' of Galley and Garland soon became a deadly combination.

Despite City's perennial fight against relegation in the Second Division, Chris' skill, selfless running and bravery was attracting the attention of scouts from the top flight. He also came to the attention of the England selectors, playing in the England Under-23s, and toured Australia with the FA representative side.

By the time the 1971/72 season started, it was obvious that City would be hard-pressed to hang onto their talented star striker and just four games – and three goals – into the season, Chris was heading for First Division giants Chelsea for £100,000.

Chris had three seasons at Stamford Bridge, scoring 22 goals for the club and playing in the League Cup final at Wembley, before moving on. 'I went to Leicester, got eight goals in ten games for them and they stayed up.' Ironically, while Chris helped Leicester to stay in the top flight, Chelsea were relegated.

After 55 games and 15 goals at Leicester, Chris 'came home', when City paid out £110,000 to bring the prodigal son back to Ashton, as they sought to preserve their First Division status. He went on to play his part in keeping the club up at the end of that 1975/76 season, but injuries restricted his appearances over the next few years, as the club plummeted down the Leagues and went into financial meltdown. As is well documented, this resulted in the 'Ashton Gate Eight', of which Chris was one, tearing up their contracts in order for Bristol City to survive. 'That was a very difficult time for all concerned – a real "can't win" situation,' Chris pointed out.

Not that this was the end of Chris in City's red and white. He made a brief comeback for them in the Fourth Division as a non-contract player, scoring the last of his 50 City goals in a 2-2 draw at Darlington – a far cry from the packed grounds of Chelsea and the like.

After soccer, Chris had an unsuccessful venture in the wine business, then went into insurance, but in 1989 was diagnosed with Parkinson's disease and has undergone surgery to alleviate the problem. 'It's a very nasty illness to cope with and it doesn't matter who you are or what you are, it can strike anybody,' said Chris, who lives in Newport with his second wife, Ruth.

Right: Chris in his Bristol City days.

Below: Chris Garland today.

DONNIE GILLIES

'Everybody remembers the goal I scored at Leeds but, in fact, there was a goal much more important than that – the one that kept us in the top flight,' says former Bristol City striker Donnie Gillies, who came to City in 1973 from Morton.

Donnie's famous match-winning goal at Elland Road came in an FA Cup replay. Having drawn 1-1 at Ashton, no one gave Second Division underdogs City much of a chance against the mighty Leeds. To the delight of the Ashton faithful, Donnie converted a through ball from Keith Fear for what proved to be the match-winner. 'To be honest we had one shot and won,' he said. 'They threw everything at us, especially after we scored – if it had been a boxing match, the referee would have stopped it!'

But, as Donnie rightly says, his equaliser at Coventry was to prove far more important. The two teams were fighting relegation from the top flight. Sunderland were also battling relegation. Due to crowd congestion – 28,000 City fans made the pilgrimage to Highfield Road – the Coventry game kicked off late, fifteen minutes after Sunderland's match.

There were all sorts of equations about who had to do what to stay up and the omens didn't look too good for City when they fell behind to the home side. Coventry scored a second, but when Gerry Gow got one for City there was hope. And when Donnie grabbed the equaliser, the fans went mad.

Both sets of fans went even wilder when the electronic scoreboard indicated that Sunderland had lost. The equation was very simple. If the score stayed the same at Highfield Road, then City and Coventry were safe and Sunderland would go down:

I've never played in a match like it. For the last fifteen minutes we just passed the ball around. Nobody from either side tried to go forward. Why risk leaving the defence exposed and letting a goal in when, if you did nothing at all and the score stayed at 2-2, we were both safe? It was an amazing game.

By 1980, with more than 200 games and 28 goals for The Robins, Donnie was on his way across town to Bristol Rovers:

When the boss rang to say Rovers wanted to sign me I wasn't that interested at first. But, as they say, they made me an offer I couldn't refuse. Ironically, if I decided against the move and stayed put, I'm sure I would have been one of the players who had to tear up their contracts when the club faced bankruptcy. There wouldn't have been an 'Ashton Gate Eight', it would have been an 'Ashton Gate Nine'.

Donnie, who had reverted to right-back in the latter half of his career, had two seasons with The Pirates, making more than 50 senior appearances, before finishing his career playing in Cyprus – ironically, where much of the fruit he now supplies with his fruit and vegetable business comes from.

These days he lives in picturesque Wells with his wife Louise. He has a daughter and two grandchildren.

Donnie in his playing days (photograph courtesy of Mike Jay).

Busy at work in his fruit and veg delivery business, Donnie Gillies today.

ERNIE HUNT

Every football club has its joker, and as characters go, they don't come much funnier than Ernie Hunt. Even his autobiography is called *Joker in the Pack*.

Ernie joined his home-town club of Swindon at fifteen. A year later he made his first-team debut against Grimsby Town. With manager Bert Head promoting the club's successful youth policy, Ernie soon established himself in the team, along with several other youngsters, such as Mike Summerbee, Bobby Woodruff and John Trollope.

'The average age of the side was nineteen and there were some very good prospects that went on to play at the top,' he pointed out. Within six years, with 239 games and 88 goals under his belt, Ernie was one of those who climbed the ladder to play top-flight football.

Wolves paid out £42,000 for Ernie and he enjoyed a two-year spell at Molineux, before the club reaped practically double their outlay by selling him to Everton for £80,000:

> I had played for England Under-23s and I knew I was on the verge of being called up to the full
> England squad, so a move to a club like Everton wasn't going to do my call-up chances any harm.
> Sadly, I was wrong. Manager Harry Catterick played me out of position on the wing, so after about
> six months I was on my way again.

A £70,000 fee took him back to the Midlands, when he signed for Coventry. Ernie was to enjoy six years with The Sky Blues, averaging roughly one goal every three games – 50 goals in 168 senior appearances. And, of course, one of those goals has gone into soccer folklore. 'Ah yes,' said Ernie with a big grin. 'The free-kick where Willie Carr flicked the ball up with his heels and I hammered it into the net.' And, just to add icing to the cake, the opposition was Everton.

A short spell on loan to Doncaster Rovers followed, and then in December 1973, Alan Dicks decided Ernie was just the sort of experienced player he needed at Ashton Gate. 'City had some very good young lads and looking around it reminded me a lot of my younger days. I suppose the younger ones looked on me as a sort of father figure,' he said.

The move to City was good for all concerned. The side benefited from Ernie's experience and undoubted skill, the crowd took to him and Ernie enjoyed the last eighteen months of his League career in City's colours. After City, Ernie moved back to the Midlands to play for non-League Atherstone. He went on to run a pub in Ledbury, spent two years looking after maladjusted children, was a painter and decorator and even had a spell as a window cleaner. 'That was alright until I fell off the ladder and broke eight ribs,' laughed Ernie.

These days Ernie, who, like many former professional footballers, has had hip replacement surgery, lives in Tredworth in Gloucester with his second wife Carol. He has two children from his first marriage and two young grandchildren.

Above: Ernie Hunt in goalscoring action.

Right: Ernie on a return to Ashton Gate to promote his autobiography.

NORMAN HUNTER

'Never meet your heroes, you'll be disappointed' – that's what some cynics say. In this author's experience that's simply not true, in fact it's quite the opposite. Having already met a number of my footballing heroes, the chance to meet up with a soccer legend – Norman 'Bite Yer Legs' Hunter – was too good to miss.

> I've got some very happy memories of my three and a half years at Bristol City. When my time was up at Leeds and they said City wanted me, I wasn't sure about the move. But when I spoke to City's (then) manager Alan Dicks and his number two Tony Collins, I knew it was the right move for me. They were very straight and upfront, the fans took to me straight away and I went on to love every minute here.

With 28 England caps (there would have been a lot more but for a certain Bobby Moore) and over 700 games for his beloved Leeds United, Norman came to City at the age of thirty-three for a £40,000 transfer fee. His brief: to keep The Robins in the top flight. To many, Norman was the hard man – he didn't get the nickname 'Bite Yer Legs' for nothing – from a very physical Leeds side that had dominated the old First Division. OK, he could tackle, but what about skill? Could he 'play'? The answer was an emphatic 'yes'. His bite in the tackle was as sharp as ever, but he soon impressed (and surprised some) fans with his ability on the ball and the quality of his passes, particularly with that cultured left foot of his.

Between 1976 and 1979 Norman notched up 113 senior appearances for City. He even weighed in with four goals. At the end of the 1978/79 season, despite having passed his mid-thirties, he was offered a two-year extension. There was even talk of him becoming player-manager. In fact he was offered the job. 'My great regret is that when I had the chance to take over from Alan Dicks I didn't take it,' he confessed. 'I felt I wasn't old enough or had sufficient experience. Looking back I regret that decision.'

An adopted Yorkshireman – Norman was actually born in Gateshead – he headed back 'home' to take up a player-coach role at Barnsley, where his old teammate Allan Clarke was in the hot seat. He went on to become manager there and when that didn't work out he moved on to take up a similar post at Rotherham.

These days, Norman is much in demand doing media work, guest appearances and after-dinner speeches, as well as being very much involved in corporate hospitality at Leeds United.

Married to Sue, he is now a sixty-one-year-old grandfather, with his two young grandsons taking up much of his time. Does he spoil them? 'Don't all grandads?' was the reply to that question.

Above: Norman (centre) during his playing days.

Right: Norman on a visit back in Bristol.

TREVOR JACOBS

Publicans and postmen seem to be the most widely chosen occupations amongst former City and Rovers players when they've finally stopped playing professional football. Former City and Rovers full-back Trevor Jacobs has tried his hand at both, and is still a postie today, covering part of the Bedminster area of Bristol.

'Running a pub was very enjoyable, although the hours were a bit unsociable,' said Trevor, who spent ten years as pub landlord, first at The Horseshoe Inn at Shepton Mallett and then The Baccy Jar in Bristol. Then he joined Royal Mail: 'I've been "on the post" now for about nineteen years and I enjoy it.'

Trevor's football career began in 1965, when he signed up as an apprentice for Bristol City. After serving his apprenticeship under manager Fred Ford, he signed professional forms in 1966, making his debut away to a Rotherham side which included John Galley and Shadow Williams. 'We were three down at half-time and I'd scored an own goal – not the best of starts,' said Trevor with a wry grin. 'On the plus side, we came back well in the second half and managed to get a draw.'

Over the next seven years, Trevor made 145 starts for the first team, scoring three goals. But in 1973, after spending a couple of months on loan to Plymouth Argyle, Trevor moved across town to the Rovers camp, which was then managed by Don Megson. 'Going from City to Rovers was never a problem for me,' he said. 'It meant I was getting regular first-team football and I didn't have to go through the upheaval of moving house and leaving the area.'

One game that Trevor is never likely to forget is his debut for Rovers:

That was against Brighton away. The telly cameras were there as it was Brian Clough's first game in charge at Brighton. Because of a mix-up over kit we had to borrow their away strip and we showed our gratitude by beating them 8–2. To say Cloughie was not best pleased would be putting it mildly. After the match he collected up the kit we borrowed and burnt it!

Trevor was to enjoy 89 games (and another three goals) at Rovers before leaving them at the end of the 1975/76 season. 'I had a season in the Western League with Bideford, but then decided to concentrate on running the pub,' he said.

These days, when Trevor has finished his post round, he can be found in his home at Bedminster. Married to Mary, the couple have two sons and three grandchildren.

Right: Trevor during his City days.

Below: Trevor today.

ANDY LLEWELLYN

Most former pro footballers remember their first senior game. It's a fair bet that nearly all of them can recall their last match. But for former Bristol City full-back Andy Llewellyn, it's his last but one game for The Robins that sticks in his mind. It was an FA Cup match for The Robins against the mighty Liverpool at Anfield, when City upset the form book and came away with a shock 1-0 win. 'Not the sort of game you're likely to forget is it?' says Andy with a smile.

Sadly for Andy, he had to serve a suspension shortly after the Anfield success, a young defender named Marvin Harriott took his place and Andy was unable to regain his first-team spot.

Two other games are also fresh in Andy's memory from his eight seasons with City – the two Freight Rover finals at Wembley. 'I was on the bench for the first game, when we beat Bolton Wanderers 3-0, and didn't get on. But the next year we were back and I was at right-back. We ended up losing on penalties to Mansfield.'

Andy's City career began as a sixteen-year-old, when he was taken onto the ground staff by then City manager Terry Cooper. He went on to play under Joe Jordan, Jimmy Lumsden, Dennis Smith and finally Russell Osman. 'It's one of those things in football that you can lose your place in the side through injury or suspension and then find that whoever's taken your place is playing well and you can't get back in,' points out Andy philosophically.

So, after around 360 games – 'and don't forget the three goals!' – Andy was on his way out of Ashton Gate. His first stop was Exeter City, where he spent a three-month loan spell, then on to Hereford United in the old Fourth Division, followed by half a season at Yeovil Town, then still a non-League side, managed by Graham Roberts.

After Yeovil Town, Andy spent five seasons in the back four at Weston-super-Mare. And he's still putting his boots on today, in his fifth season as player-manager for Clevedon United in the Western League.

Away from the football field, Andy, like many of his former colleagues, earns his living as a postman:

> Once you get used to the early starts it's not too bad and, just like in my pro days, the afternoons are your own. It's also quite rewarding at this time of the year (December) because as well as the gas bills, bank statements and advertising mail, you're also delivering festive greetings to people from family and friends, some of whom live miles away, which is nice, although it does make it a very busy time for everyone at Royal Mail.

Right: Andy in action during his City days.

Below: Getting the Christmas mail through with Royal Mail.

KEVIN MABBUTT

When Kevin Mabbutt finished his playing days, he decided to make a complete break. So, after a short spell in the commercial property business, the former Bristol City star striker headed for the USA, where he is now the manager of a top-class restaurant.

> My father-in-law opened the restaurant Delicias after he moved out to California fifteen years ago. After playing football I decided I didn't want to go into coaching or soccer management, so when the chance came to start a new life in America, I jumped at it. The climate is terrific – there's no humidity there and the lifestyle is very good.

One of the three footballing Mabbutts – dad Ray is a Rovers legend and brother Gary found fame with Rovers, Spurs and England – Kevin made his debut for City against Nottingham Forest in the First Division in 1977. He scored his first senior goal for the club against Villa a few weeks later and went on to make 13 appearances while still only eighteen years old.

One of football's 'naturals', the young striker was soon establishing himself in City's red and white with his speed, skill and eye for goal. He once got the better of internationals Gordon McQueen and Martin Buchan by scoring a hat-trick at Old Trafford.

By the end of his first season, Kevin had featured in 37 senior games, which included winning the Anglo-Scottish Cup. Over his four seasons with City, he was well on the way to 200 appearances and nearly half a century of goals.

Sadly, by the end of the 1979/80 season, City's top-flight dream was over. And when they went down again the following season, it was always on the cards that Kevin was destined to play at a higher level, especially as City's financial situation was beginning to spiral towards a major crisis. In October 1981, with City struggling in the Third Division, Kevin moved back up the Leagues with a move to Crystal Palace, in exchange for much-needed cash – £100,000 – plus Palace defender Terry Boyle.

Between 1981 and 1985, Kevin played 75 games for The Eagles, scoring 22 goals. But a succession of niggling pelvic and knee injuries spelt the end of Kevin's career as a professional footballer:

> Bristol City was a very important part of my life and I still look out for their results. The management, players, staff and fans played vital roles in the club's successful years and hopefully that success will come back.

As well as regularly checking the results from back home, Kevin has also not lost touch completely with the soccer scene: 'We get quite a lot of football fans come to the restaurant and, in addition, customers have included former Spurs stars Richard Gough and Jurgen Klinsman, as well as City old boy Gary Collier.'

Married to Lisa, the couple have three young daughters, Jessica, Isabel and Milly.

Kevin during his playing days.

Kevin, with wife Lisa and
sister-in-law Kathy (left).

MIKE MAHONEY

From Bristol to Torquay, Torquay to Newcastle, Newcastle to the United States and back – no one could ever accuse Mike Mahoney of being afraid to move in pursuit of his chosen career. In fact, Mike was always on the move, whether he was racing off his goal line to save at the feet of an oncoming striker or heading for the motorway or airport to join his next club.

'Yes, you could say I've been around,' said Mike, just after he'd appeared 'between the sticks' in a charity match for the Bristol City Legends team.

Born in Bristol in 1950, Mike joined Bristol City as an apprentice in 1968, but, despite showing plenty of promise and ability, Mike Gibson had made the goalkeeper's position his own at Ashton Gate and, after just a handful of games, Mahoney sought regular first-team action at Torquay United. There Mike came into his own, playing over 200 games between 1970 and 1975. A firm favourite with The Gulls' fans, Mike's agility in goal eventually attracted scouts from the higher Leagues and in 1975 he made the step up to the top flight, signing for Newcastle United:

> That was a great move for me. The fans up there are marvellous, wonderful people. You'd probably get over 30,000 turn up just to watch the shirts dry on the washing line!

A brave goalkeeper who cared little for his own personal safety (well they do say all goalkeepers are mad), Mike endeared himself to the Geordie fans. 'Mike was not only an excellent goalkeeper, but as tough as old boots,' recalled my northern correspondent Gerry McReynolds. 'I remember a UEFA Cup match against Bohemians in Dublin when Mike got hit by a heavy object thrown by the crowd. He still played a blinder.'

In 1979, Mike joined the soccer exodus to the USA, signing up for the Chicago Stings to play in the West America Soccer League. 'Soccer, although not of the highest standard, was really catching on in the States and a lot of ex-pats and big-name players – such as George Best, Franz Beckenbauer and Rodney Marsh – made the move,' he said.

After the Chicago Stings, Mike moved on to the California Surfs, where he spent six years, before taking up a coaching job in indoor soccer in Los Angeles. 'After a couple of years of that I had to get "a proper job",' recalled Mike with a laugh. 'I spent a lot of time delivering beer for the Miller Brewing Company.' Not that Mike ever came across much Newcastle Brown Ale!

> I only intended going out there for two years and ended up staying for twenty-three – I loved it there. The trouble was we wanted to see more of our daughter Trudi and our two grandchildren, so we came back.

These days Mike and his wife Janet live in the St George area of Bristol. And Mike's still 'on the move' – he works in the transport department of the Post Office.

Right: Mike in goalkeeping action.

Below: Taking the field for a charity football match for the Bristol City Legends.

GARY MARSHALL

Politicians – they're never out of the news. So who better to give an opinion on the make-up of the cabinet than former Bristol City winger Gary Marshall. After all, he is a cabinet maker! 'I served an apprenticeship as a cabinet maker before signing for City. In fact, I turned down the chance to sign as a full-time pro for them so that I could complete the apprenticeship.'

With a trade safely under his belt, Gary duly signed on for the City in 1983, making his debut against Derby County. 'I managed to get a goal in my first game, which wasn't a bad way to start,' he recalled.

After five years and over 60 senior appearances for The Robins, Gary moved on to Carlisle United. 'Clive Middlemass, who had been Terry Cooper's number two at City, was the manager at Carlisle and that was probably the main reason why I signed for them,' he said. 'With hindsight, it was a bad move. The club was run on a shoestring and was always struggling financially.'

After two seasons at Carlisle, Gary moved on again. This time his destination was Scunthorpe United. 'Now that was a good move,' he said. 'Scunthorpe had just moved into a brand new ground and had put together a pretty decent side – I loved it there.'

With Terry Cooper installed as the manager at Exeter City and looking for a winger as part of his team-building plans, Gary couldn't resist the chance to return to the South West, ending an eighteen-month stay with 'The Iron' to come 'back home'. 'It was fine while Terry was there, but when he left it wasn't the same,' pointed out Gary.

With one or two footballing injuries catching up with him, Gary decided to end his two and a half year spell at St James' Park and quit the professional game at the age of twenty-nine. 'I turned out for Paulton and Clevedon Town for a while and also got involved in coaching a local junior team, which was very rewarding,' said Gary.

Looking back, what were his best and worst memories of playing for Bristol City?

> The year we first played in the Freight Rover final at Wembley was so frustrating. It was great that we won (3-0 against Bolton) but I was on the subs' bench and didn't get on. We went back the following year and I was in the line-up this time. Although we eventually lost in a penalty shoot-out, it was a wonderful experience to play on Wembley's hallowed turf – every footballer's dream.

Gary now lives in Worle, with his second wife Linda. He has two children from his first marriage and three stepchildren.

Above: Gary (right) in League action against Plymouth Argyle.

Right: Cabinet maker Gary, busy in his Blagdon workshop.

PETER McCALL

One of the main ingredients of having a successful football team is finding the right chemistry. Former Bristol City wing half Peter McCall may not have won any FA Cup medals, but the chemistry is not a problem – these days he works for a pharmacist! 'I'm employed by Siddalls Pharmacy, delivering to health centres, nursing homes and so on,' explained Peter.

Born in West Ham in 1936, Peter was spotted playing for Kings Lynn by a Bristol City scout. Having joined The Robins in 1952, his City career was almost over before it begun. 'In just my second game I broke my ankle playing for City Colts', he explained. Peter then had to endure five months out of action.

After biding his time and learning his trade in the reserves, Peter finally made his debut in a 3–2 Good Friday win at Cardiff. The following day he kept his place in the side that drew 3–3 with arch rivals Bristol Rovers and two days later, the Easter Monday, he was on the team sheet once again for the return match with Cardiff, which brought a 2–0 win. He kept his place in the side for the rest of the season.

Over a nine-year spell, Peter clocked up 84 senior appearances, finding the net once – in a 3–0 home win over Brighton at the beginning of the 1958/59 season. Centre half and colleague Alan Williams had joined Oldham Athletic in 1961 and a year later Peter left Ashton Gate to follow his friend's route up north. 'They were looking for a wing half and I think Alan recommended me, which was nice. Also, it was reassuring going to a new club to find a familiar face there,' he said.

Peter had three seasons with The Latics, playing alongside Alan. Both were in the Oldham side that lost 2–0 to City in the last match of the 1964/65 season – City's win earning them promotion from the old Third Division. 'It was quite strange going back to Ashton Gate to play them in what was such an important game,' confessed Peter.

In 1966 Peter packed his bags and left Oldham to join Hereford United in the Southern League, giving him the chance to move back to Bristol. 'They were lovely people up there, but my wife didn't really settle and we'd always planned to come back to this area,' explained Peter.

Approaching the end of his playing days, Peter first got a job at a local builder's merchants located in the shadow of the Ashton Gate floodlights, and then, eleven years later, worked for the local council.

An all-rounder, Peter was also no slouch at tennis and cricket, although it was at bowls that he went on to excel after hanging up his soccer boots and for four years he played for the England bowls team.

Married to Joan for over forty years, the couple live in Long Ashton and have two sons, a daughter and four grandchildren.

Above: Peter (second left) in pre-season action against Bristol Rovers.

Right: Getting those deliveries out to the health centres and nursing homes.

GEOFF MERRICK

A League debut at seventeen, captain of his local side at the age of twenty and skipper of the team that finally won promotion to the top flight. There was even talk of transfer interest by the big clubs, including the mighty Arsenal, and the possibility of an England call-up was not entirely out of the question. It was all going too well for former England Schoolboy international Geoff Merrick.

And so it was to prove. Six years after the joys of leading his club into the First Division and over thirteen years after making his City debut, Geoff became one of the 'Ashton Gate Eight', who tore up their contracts so that financially crippled Bristol City could survive.

A natural left-footer and an excellent leader on the field, Geoff could mark the most gifted opposition striker out of a match with his decisive tackles, heading skills and ability to read the game.

Just 5ft 9ins tall, Geoff made the first of 427 senior starts in a 4-2 win at Aston Villa in May 1968, at the age of seventeen. Over the next two seasons he was to make a couple of dozen appearances, but, come the end of the 1971/72 season, he was an ever-present, making the no.6 shirt his own. It was to stay that way until the autumn of 1976 saw the arrival of Norman Hunter and Geoff moved to the left-back position.

After four seasons in the top division and despite Geoff's total commitment to the cause, the club began a downward plummet through the divisions, while at the same time living above their means. All of this meant a tremendous sacrifice for the eight senior players, including Geoff, who agreed to leave in order to keep the club alive financially.

After leaving City, Geoff played in Hong Kong and South Africa, before seeing out his playing days in the non-League scene back home. 'When I finished playing I decided I didn't want to go into coaching or management,' said Geoff. 'I did a bit of farming for a couple of years, then got involved in the building and maintenance trade and now run my own company – GMS Multi Services.'

Now in his fifties, Geoff lives in Nailsea with his wife Wendy. The couple have two sons and a daughter.

We did a lot of good things at Bristol City and most of the lads who left to save the club were involved in getting them into the top flight. It's just unfortunate that we'll probably always be remembered most for being the 'Ashton Gate Eight'.

Above: Geoff (front row, third from right) in the 1975/76 City squad.

Right: Geoff the builder today.

RALPH MILNE

He's got two League Cup winners' medals, two Scottish Cup runners-up medals and one Premier League medal. What's more, his great-grandfather wrote *Winnie the Pooh*. We're talking about Ralph Milne, former star of Dundee United, Charlton Athletic, Bristol City and Manchester United. Also, the great-grandson of author A.A. Milne.

Dundee born and bred – 'and proud of it' – Ralph spent ten years with Dundee United, picking up his League Cup and Scottish Cup runners-up medals in the process. He clocked up 272 senior games for The Arabs, scoring 72 goals, an average of one in four – not bad for someone who spent most of his time on the wing. During their European adventures, he also bagged 15 goals in 35 games, a record unlikely to be beaten.

In 1987, Ralph moved 'down south', when Lenny Lawrence agreed a £125,000 transfer fee to take him to Charlton Athletic in the old First Division. After a year playing for Charlton at Selhurst Park, Ralph moved on to the West Country, joining the Terry Cooper revival at Bristol City on a month's loan:

> That was quite odd. I came down on loan, along with Steve McClaren, now the England boss. Towards the end of the loan period we signed contracts with City and the very next day Terry Cooper left the club!

Cooper was replaced by Joe Jordan and Ralph was to enjoy success on the wing, as Joe's team pushed hard for promotion. They eventually reached the Third Division play-offs, finally losing out in a mammoth struggle with Walsall. But, as one door closes, another one opens:

> Obviously we were all gutted to lose in the play-offs, but later Joe called me in to say they'd had an offer for me – from Manchester United. My first reaction was that it was some sort of wind-up, but apparently Sir Alex had watched me play in the Walsall game and United then offered City £175,000 to take me to Old Trafford.

After two and a half years at United, Ralph was off to join the soccer exodus to Hong Kong. 'That was another great experience,' he recalls. 'There were a lot of ex-Pats there, which made settling in quite easy. It also meant we could socialise together, which was nice.'

After a year playing for Sing Tao, Ralph had the chance of another twelve months, but decided to come home: 'To tell you the truth, the legs had started to go and I didn't think I could do the side justice.'

'I've had a great career,' sums up Ralph, who has spent the last twelve years in the licensed trade. 'I've played all over the world and had some wonderful times. I suppose you could say that, coming from Dundee, I've been able to have my Dundee cake and eat it – and I don't even like cake!'

Right: Ralph in goalscoring action for Dundee.

Below: From telling passes to pulling pints, former City star Ralph Milne.

ARTHUR MILTON

The last sportsman to play football and cricket for England was Arthur Milton, who played cricket six times for England and once for the England football team, back in the 1950s. What's more, he finished his illustrious soccer career playing for Bristol City.

Arthur had been spotted playing football on the Downs by an Arsenal scout. Signing for The Gunners, he progressed through Arsenal's third and second teams, fitting in the then compulsory National Service, before getting the 'call-up' he really wanted – to Arsenal's first team. 'I made my debut for them against Villa on my twenty-third birthday,' recalled Arthur.

Arthur's skill on the wing soon caught the attention of the England selectors and he got his international call-up to the side that played Austria at Wembley in the 1952/53 season. And it wasn't just his skills with a football that brought him to the attention of the England selectors. One of those band of sportsmen who combined soccer and cricket, his all-round ability on the cricket field for Gloucester earned him a call-up to the international cricket team. 'I made my debut against New Zealand at Headingley in 1958 and managed 104 not out,' said Arthur. Not a bad start.

Having played 84 games and scored 21 goals for Arsenal, Arthur left the club in February 1955, answering a call from City manager Pat Beasley to return 'home' and sign for Bristol City. 'I knew Pat from my days at Arsenal and, after a chat, I said I'd join them for the rest of the season, but would probably give up football to concentrate on my cricket after that,' he explained. Even on that short-term basis, it cost The Robins £4,000 (a tidy sum in those days) to bring him to Ashton Gate.

Short-term the transfer may have been, but Arthur was certainly value for money. He played in City's last 14 games, scored three times and never finished on the losing side. What's more, he played a major role in helping them win promotion as champions from the old Third Division (South):

> There were some very good players at City – Ivor Guy, Tommy Burden and, of course, John Atyeo – but my mind was made up to concentrate on cricket and I left professional football at the end of that season.

Arthur went on to enjoy many seasons at Gloucester and was still playing cricket at the age of forty-six. 'I'd always enjoyed sport – it was never about the money. In fact, the wages were not particularly good, so small, in fact, I can't even remember what I used to get!' he said with a laugh.

Away from the sports fields, Arthur became a familiar face in the Sneyd Park area of Bristol, delivering the post for Royal Mail, before retiring nineteen years ago. Married to his wife Joan for more than fifty years, the couple, who live in Henleaze, have three sons and six grandchildren.

Arthur, in his playing days for Bristol City.

All-rounder Arthur Milton, still the centre of media attention today.

SID MORGAN

'Goalkeepers today? They're nothing more than glorified ballet dancers – they don't know they're born!' That's the verdict of former City custodian Sid Morgan:

> You can't go within two yards of a keeper these days without the ref giving a free-kick. Crikey, in my day, it was nothing to catch the ball and end up in the back of the net still holding the ball, courtesy of some strapping big centre forward who made sure you and the ball ended up in the net. And the referee would give a goal!

OK, so goalies today are just a little bit overprotected compared to Sid's time in the game. Signed from Downs League side AFC Farmer, Sid joined Bristol City in December 1947. 'Although I'd played in goal for school and services teams, I was playing full-back for AFC Farmer when they decided, after a 7-7 draw, to change the keeper and so I put on the green jersey,' he recalled. His performances for the team soon attracted the attention of Bristol City and Sid was on his way to The Robins.

Sid made his first-team debut for The Robins in March 1949, a 2-0 victory at Torquay United in what was the old Third Division South. He made nine appearances between the sticks that season and 18 the following year. At the start of the 1950/51 season, Sid claimed the number one spot, playing in the first 19 games. But then Con Sullivan got the nod and was an ever-present for the next year and a half, before moving on to Arsenal. Back came Sid for ten games, before losing out again, this time to the late Tony Cook. Ironically, like Sid, Con and Tony had also been spotted playing on the Downs.

'There were some very good keepers in my time at City and also injuries restricted the number of matches I played,' said Sid. With 73 senior games behind him, Sid moved on to sign for Millwall. 'Jimmy Seed, who'd had a spell as caretaker manager at City, was the Millwall boss, so he knew all about me and vice versa,' he explained.

Sid had the best part of two seasons at Millwall, but a bad injury, highlighting the under-protection of goalkeepers back then, brought an end to his career:

> We were playing at Coventry and the centre forward came through and caught me. I managed to play on, but it was days afterwards that they found I had broken ribs, which had punctured a lung. I wouldn't mind, but I got a rollicking from the boss for letting a goal in!

After a week in hospital, Sid came out to look for a new career and went on to become an electrician until his retirement. 'I've had cartilage problems, damaged ligaments, broken ribs and a punctured lung, to name a few of the knocks I picked up – and that was par for the course for a goalie in those days. We didn't have no ballet dancers in goal then!' summed up Sid with a laugh.

Right: Sid in his playing days.

Below: Sid gets to meet Sir Trevor Brooking at the recent Downs League 100th anniversary celebrations.

RUSSELL MUSKER

If you're a professional footballer, you never know what's around the corner. One minute you're on top of your form and attracting scouts from the top division, the next minute you could be stretchered off with a career-threatening injury. And that's what happened to Russell Musker.

A talented young player who was making an impact in City's midfield, he broke his leg in seven places on the day that a Spurs scout had come to watch him. Russell's unlucky break came in 1981 in a League match against Swindon. 'They told me that I'd never play again, but I wasn't having that. After an eternity on the injured list, I came back.'

An amiable bloke, Russell is fondly remembered by officials of most of the clubs he was with, notably City, Gillingham, Torquay United and Taunton Town.

It was in 1977 that Russell joined City as an apprentice. He made his debut against Chelsea in the 1979/80 season, going on to notch up nearly 60 senior appearances for The Robins. Not that goalscoring was his strong point at City, with just one goal to his credit. 'Yes, but what a goal it was — a left-foot volley against Hull at Ashton Gate, that their keeper didn't even see,' Russell pointed out.

Transferred to Gillingham in November 1983, Russell made almost 100 starts for The Gills. 'I had three very enjoyable years there,' recalled Russell. Devon was his next port of call. 'I had two years with Torquay as a player, but then the old war wounds caught up with me and I was put in charge of the YTS scheme there,' said Russell. 'Later, I became assistant manager to Dave Smith — a lovely chap.'

A short spell at Walsall didn't work out, before Russell dropped out of the League with moves to Gloucester City and Weymouth.

A born leader, nobody was surprised when Russell turned to soccer management, taking the hot seat at Taunton Town. He went on to give sterling service to the club over an eleven-year period and became the most successful manager in the club's history before stepping down. 'We won the Screwfix League five times, the Somerset Premier Cup and, best of all, the FA Vase at Villa Park,' he said proudly.

Such is the esteem that Russell is held in at Taunton, that when he decided to step down, the club made him an honorary life member. Living in Torquay, Russell spends much of his time as a self-employed property developer in Devon.

Football is about getting the breaks. I've had some great times and wonderful memories. The one break I could have done without was that leg break at City!

Right: Russell during his playing days.

Below: Russell Musker today.

STUART NAYLOR

Most people get a greetings card on Valentine's Day. Former City goalkeeper got an 'I want you' message of a different kind – a dream move from the Fourth Division to the top flight with West Bromwich Albion:

> I was with Lincoln City and initially was on my way to Birmingham City. Just before the deal was completed the Birmingham manager – Ron Saunders – got the sack. I thought that was that, but Ron went on to manage West Brom and I became his first signing – on Valentine's Day of all days.

Stuart had joined Lincoln as a seventeen-year-old. 'The youth team manager was Lennie Lawrence and he was a very big influence on my career,' said Stuart.

During his time with The Imps, Stuart saw plenty of first-team action, as well as having loan spells with Crewe Alexandra and Peterborough United. 'Peterborough's first-team goalie was a certain David Seaman and when he got injured I was brought in as cover,' recalled Stuart.

But Valentine's Day 1986 saw Stuart head for the Midlands and the chance to play against the country's best. 'I think ambition is very important and to get the opportunity to play at the highest level is what it's all about,' he said.

Having already played for the England Youth team, Stuart was delighted to get selected for an England 'B' team that included the likes of Paul Gascoigne, David Platt and Steve Bull. 'We toured Iceland, Norway and Switzerland,' said Stuart. 'I've never experienced cold like it. Iceland was cold with a capital 'C'- it was like playing on the moon.'

After ten years with West Brom, Stuart was heading to the south west to sign for Bristol City. 'Joe Jordan was the manager there at the time and the regular goalkeeper was involved in a contract dispute, so he brought me in,' pointed out Stuart.

A change of manager and a spell out injured meant that Stuart moved on from City. He had two months at Walsall and by the summer of 1999 he was set to sign for non-League Weymouth Town. 'I played for them in a pre-season fixture against Exeter City and had a decent enough game. Shortly afterwards Exeter's keeper was injured and their manager remembered my performance and asked me to sign for them instead,' said Stuart. 'Fred Davies, the Weymouth manager understood that it was a chance for me to stay in the League and didn't stand in my way.'

After nearly a year at Exeter, another management change saw Stuart contemplating moving on. He answered an SOS from Brian Talbot, formerly with West Brom and the boss at Conference League Rushden & Diamonds. After narrowly missing out on promotion to the Football League in his first season there, Stuart took on the dual role of goalkeeper and goalkeeping coach and played a key role in helping his side achieve Football League status, which, sadly, they have since lost.

After his time at Rushden, Stuart returned to Ashton Gate to take on the role of coaching City's goalkeepers. He lives in the Long Ashton area of Bristol.

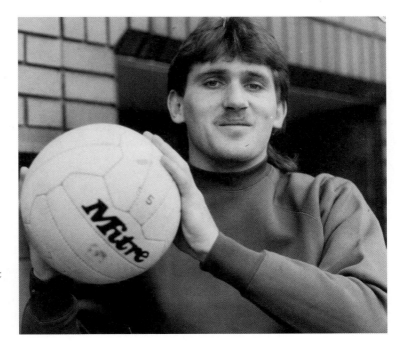

Right: Goalkeeper Stuart Naylor in his playing days.

Below: Stuart today.

ROB NEWMAN

One of the most popular and dependable players to put on a Bristol City shirt, Rob Newman experienced just about every gambit of football life at Ashton Gate: relegation, promotion (twice), and two Freight Rover Trophy finals at Wembley. A City veteran with nearly 500 senior appearances by the age of twenty-eight, Rob Newman's been there, done it and got the T-shirt.

Born in Bradford-on-Avon, Rob joined City as an apprentice in 1980. By February 1982 he was among a clutch of youngsters pitched into the first team, following the financial crisis that saw eight of the club's senior players tear up their contracts in order for the club to survive. The departure of the 'Ashton Gate Eight' did mean that young reserves like Rob were given their first-team chance earlier than planned and he went on to make 15 senior appearances, plus eight as sub, although the side still plunged into the Fourth Division.

The following year Rob was virtually an ever-present, as manager Terry Cooper stabilised the sinking ship to finish in mid-table. 'Terry was fantastic for Bristol City and for me personally,' said Rob. 'He created a tremendous team spirit and I still ring him to ask his advice to this day.'

A versatile player, Rob featured at full-back, centre half, midfield and even up front. 'It's true, I played all over the place, which usually meant I was in the starting line up, as there was usually someone suspended or injured,' he said.

Rob went on to play a pivotal role in City's rise from the ashes and was a key player in City gaining promotion back to Division Three. There was also the Freight Rover Trophy success.

By the end of the 1990/91 season Rob had been an ever-present in the side for three years, clocked up nearly 500 games and scored 61 goals. Twice he'd played at Wembley and he'd gone on to captain the side, something he considered 'a great honour.'

A move to the top flight was always on the cards and in 1991 he packed his bags and headed for Anglia as Norwich City paid The Robins £600,000 for his services. He passed the 200 mark for The Canaries in his seven years there, had loan spells at Wigan and Motherwell, before moving on to Southend United, where he played 72 times. When the chance came to take over the manager's job at Roots Hall, he took it, although agrees it probably came too soon for him.

As is the way of soccer management, a run of bad results saw Rob and Southend part company. He went on to manage Cambridge United and latterly became assistant manager at Bournemouth.

'I've played under a lot of managers in my career and would like to think I've learnt something from all them, even the bad ones,' said Rob, who lives with his wife Joanne and four-year-old daughter Harriott in Norfolk.

Above: Rob (top right) enjoying an after-match soak in the communal bath.

Right: Rob Newman today.

RUSSELL OSMAN

There was no doubting Russell Osman's pedigree, when he came to Ashton Gate in October 1991. Nearly 400 games for a successful Ipswich Town side in the late 1970s and early '80s, he also played over 100 games for Leicester City and a similar amount for Southampton. In addition, he had represented England at Youth, Under-21 and full international (11 games) level. He was also one of a star-studded line-up of players who had parts in the 1981 film, *Escape to Victory*.

> We didn't have a bad side in the film did we? Mike Summerbee, Bobby More, Ossie Ardilles, Pele... not a bad side at all, although I don't think I'd want Michael Caine or Sylvester Stallone in one of my teams! It was a great experience and good fun. We had five weeks in Budapest, and the filming came just after we (Ipswich) had won the UEFA Cup – one of my fondest memories.

It was in 1991 that Russell came to City, having spent the previous three years with The Saints, making his debut in a home victory over Watford. Virtually an ever-present for the next two seasons, Russell took over as player-manager in 1993, succeeding Dennis Smith. But the only fairly certain thing about football management is that it's not a job for life. And, after a few bad results, Russell, who had notched up 130 games for The Robins, and City parted company in 1995. 'As a football manager you know you're on a hiding to nothing, but that's the nature of the beast,' said Russell philosophically.

After City, Russell wore the colours of Brighton & Hove Albion and Cardiff City, was caretaker manager at Plymouth and then returned to Cardiff as manager. After a spell away from the game, he answered an SOS from Bristol Rovers, a club going through a managerial crisis and staring relegation to the Conference in the face. Russell's brief was to take on the role of caretaker-manager and keep the club in the League. He did.

After helping Rovers to stay up, Russell returned to doing media work and is a regular on Eurosport, Today FM and ITV West. And, when he's not on the airwaves, Russell, an avid golfer, can be usually found at least once a week on the nearest golf course. 'As a footballer you get a lot of spare time. I wasn't into card schools or gambling (the downfall of many a footballer) so I got into golf, which I love,' explained Russell. And he's not ruled out a return to football management – 'you never know when the phone might ring,' he pointed out.

Russell and his wife live in picturesque Tockington. They have a teenage son Tom and teenage twins Ben and Toby.

Above: Russell Osman, in action for City.

Left: Tee time for Russell on the golf course.

GORDON PARR

There can't be too many Bristol City players who spend practically all of their playing careers at Ashton Gate and leave on 'a free' to join a club which had just qualified for the European Cup. But that's exactly what happened to City wing half Gordon Parr, who departed from Ashton Gate in 1972 to join Irish champions Waterford.

> I'd never 'done' Ireland before, but after leaving City, the chance to rub shoulders with Europe's finest was too good to turn down. The team was managed by ex-Man United defender Shay Brennan and, in addition to taking part in the European Cup, we also toured America. Not a bad way to finish!

Gordon began his City career in 1957, having captained Bristol Schoolboys and trialled for the England Schoolboys team. One of the fittest players on City's books, Gordon started off in the reserves: 'It was a good education and if we were playing against the likes of Arsenal or Spurs reserves, we'd get crowds of 3,000 or more.' It wasn't until the early 1960s that Gordon established a place in City's first team and was soon forming a formidable partnership with centre half Jack Connor in the heart of City's defence. His commitment and solid, no-nonsense performances were a key factor in the side gaining promotion from the Third Division in 1965.

For the next five seasons Gordon was virtually an ever-present, and although City were usually to be found fighting relegation, they did enjoy some decent cup runs. He was a member of the side that lost 2-0 to Spurs at White Hart Lane in March 1967, a result that could have been so different if City hadn't missed a twice-taken penalty.

At the end of the 1971/72 season manager Alan Dicks, who had replaced Fred Ford in the Ashton 'hot seat' in 1967, decided that it was time to let Gordon go. He'd notched up well over 300 senior appearances and scored four goals – well, he was more renowned for his defensive abilities than his goalscoring prowess. And his fifteen years' loyal service did not go unrewarded, with City setting up a testimonial fund for their long-serving stalwart.

For many, that could have spelt the end of a professional soccer career, but Gordon's loyalty and dedication was rewarded with his 'Irish adventure': 'I really enjoyed it and the beauty of it was I didn't even have to leave Bristol, as it was agreed that I would fly over regularly from Lullsgate Airport.'

After Ireland, Gordon played out his football career with Western League side Minehead. Having served an apprenticeship as an electrician, he went on to build a successful career as an electrical contractor. Married to Sheila, they have one daughter, Samantha, and a young grandson, Oliver.

Right: In action for City.

Below: All wired up, light work for Gordon today.

SCOTT PARTRIDGE

It was always a fair possibility that Scott Partridge would break into professional football. His dad, Malcolm, was a goalscoring striker who numbered Grimsby Town, Leicester City, Scunthorpe United, Chesterfield and Mansfield Town among the clubs he regularly found the net for.

Born in Leicester, Scott was spotted as a fourteen-year-old by a Bradford City scout and signed YTS forms for The Bantams. In his two-and-a-half years at Valley Parade, Scott made over a dozen first-team appearances. 1993/94 saw him join Bristol City and, over the next three years he notched up over half a century of senior games. 'Russell Osman signed me for City,' said Scott. 'They had some very good players there – Mark Shail, Rob Edwards, Brian Tinnion and Wayne "The Chief" Allison, who I particularly enjoyed playing up front with.'

Scott also enjoyed loan spells at Torquay United and Plymouth Argyle, before another transfer saw him lining up in the (old) Third Division with Cardiff City. The move over 'the bridge' didn't work out though. 'I have to admit, it wasn't one of my best moves and I was glad to leave,' admitted Scott.

A 40-game spell at Torquay went better and, with 15 goals under his belt, Scott was again under the watchful eyes of visiting scouts. A £100,000 bid was hard for Torquay to resist and Scott was on his way to Griffin Park, home of Brentford. 'I had two-and-a-half years there, followed by another two-and-a-half at Rushden & Diamonds. That was quite exciting as it coincided with their first season in the Football League,' said Scott.

Knowing that his full-time footballing days were drawing to close, Scott decided that he would take up plumbing as a living. He attended college in order to learn the trade and get his qualifications.

Dropping out of the League, Scott had six months at Steve Claridge's Weymouth. 'That was another one that didn't go well and I was glad to get away and sign for Bath City,' pointed out Scott. It was at Bath that Scott really rediscovered his scoring form, making him a favourite among the Twerton faithful. In fact, it was his goalscoring that saw him make a surprise return to the Millennium Stadium:

> I'd played there twice before – for Brentford in the LDV Trophy and for Rushden in the play-offs – and lost both times. I'd never actually seen an FA Cup final live, but the FA and the TV people were running a competition asking members of the public to nominate players who had made an impact in FA Cup matches that season. I'd got a hat-trick in a third-round tie at Broadhurst and that got me the votes.

These days Scott is still finding the back of the net regularly for Bath City. Married to Caroline, the couple live in Wraxall with their two young children Lauren and Harvey.

Lining up for Bristol City.

Plumbing's 'no wrench' for Scott!

ROGER PETERS

'The best goal I ever scored?' Former City winger Roger 'Lou' Peters thought for a few minutes:

> It was one of two. One was in an FA Cup match at Halifax. We were losing 1-0 when we broke away on the right. I found myself running through the middle and as it came over I suddenly thought to myself, 'Oh dear, I've got to head it'. I didn't get many goals with my head, but on this occasion I caught it perfectly and it beat their keeper all ends up. We got the draw and won the replay.

A speedy winger equally at home on either flank, Lou netted a total of 27 goals during his eight-year City career. In fact, one season his 11 goals made him the club's top scorer. So what was the other goal that sticks in his mind?

> That was at Bolton. They had an England international in goal called Eddie Hopkinson. 'Big' John (Atyeo) nodded the ball back to me on the edge of the box and I hit it first time to find the top corner of the net.

Roger made his City debut in the 1960/61 season on his seventeenth birthday. He went on to make 176 senior appearances in City's colours:

> The manager, Fred Ford, was a great guy. You won't find anyone who's played for Fred who has got a bad word to say about the man. He called a spade a spade and could dish out a rollicking when necessary, but once he said his piece that was that. He'd put his arm around you and buy you a drink ten minutes later.
>
> John Atyeo was another who was very special. Not only was he a great player, but he had charisma. And when John had something to say, you listened. I remember travelling back after a defeat at Carlisle. Those were the days before motorways and super deluxe coaches. A trip to Carlisle and back, especially the return trip if you'd been beaten, was not something you looked forward to. But after a few miles John starting chatting about football – his matches for England and the players he played with – and the journey didn't seem half as long.

Roger himself has worn the white shirt of England, playing for the England Youth team against Israel. 'There were some very good players in that side,' he said. 'There was Jim Montgomery in goal, Leicester's Graham Cross, George Armstrong from Arsenal and Martin Peters. I made out to local journalists that Martin was my brother!'

In 1968 Roger left City to try his luck on the coast at Bournemouth. He had two seasons there before coming back to the area to finish his footballing days at Bath City. He went on to work in insurance for thirty years, before setting himself up as an independent financial advisor. Married to Joyce, the couple live on the seafront at Clevedon. They have two daughters and two grandchildren.

Above: Lou Peters (right) in action at Ashton Gate.

Right: Lou today, arriving home at Clevedon.

HOWARD PRITCHARD

One thing you could never accuse former Bristol City winger Howard Pritchard of was lacking drive. In two spells and nearly 200 games with The Robins he could 'motor' down that right wing, setting up chances for one of his teammates or hitting home one of the 30 goals he bagged for them. So it shouldn't come as any surprise that driving is what he does today. 'I've got a full HGV Class I License, a PSV (Public Service Vehicle) Class I License and I run my own driving school,' he said. 'I was conscious towards the end of my career that I needed to look to my future and driving appealed.'

Looking back, Howard has no problem remembering the last time he wore the red and white of Bristol City back in 1986. It was the Freight Rover Trophy final at Wembley, when City triumphed 3-0 over Bolton Wanderers; Howard had a blinder and scored one of the goals. 'I suppose you could say I left on a bit of a high note,' he says with a laugh.

Born in Cardiff, another of Howard's 'high notes' was being selected for the full Welsh international side, lining up alongside the likes of Mark Hughes and Ian Rush in a 1-1 draw with Norway.

Howard had joined City as an apprentice in 1975/76 – the season they went up to the old First Division. He enjoyed life on the wing when selected, but moved on to Swindon Town at the end of the 1980/81 season, where he was to spend two seasons and notch up 29 goals. In 1983 it was back 'home' to City, who by now were dropping down the divisions. 'I actually played in all four divisions for them,' he points out.

After their Freight Rover success Howard decided to move on. 'To tell the truth I couldn't agree new terms,' he explains. 'There were a lot of new players coming in on much better money than I was getting, and I didn't think that was right.'

A £22,000 transfer fee saw him moving to Keith Peacock's Gillingham. Two seasons later he was on the move again, linking up with former City star Gerry Sweeney who was the assistant manager at Walsall. His final League move saw him signing for Maidstone, then in the Football League. 'I had fifteen months there and left just before the club went bankrupt,' he recalls.

He went on to link up with another City old boy, Clive Whitehead, who was in charge at Yeovil, then still a non-League side, where he enjoyed a year and a half, before deciding it was time to look outside of the game for his future.

Today Howard still has that same dedication that brought about those happy memories, although these days it's not about his defence-splitting passes, but more about getting his pupils driving test passes.

Former City outside right Howard Pritchard.

Ready for the road and another driving lesson.

GLYN RILEY

Barnsley-born Glyn Riley arrived at Bristol City in the summer of 1982, in the aftermath of the club's disastrous slide down the divisions and near financial extinction. There weren't many smiles on the faces of the Ashton Gate faithful in those dark days, but Glyn's goalscoring exploits and affinity with the fans soon changed all that. 'Terry (Cooper) brought me down from Barnsley and despite the fact that I'd only been married two weeks, we settled in very well,' said Glyn.

Glyn's football career began with his home-town club and he made his debut for Barnsley at the age of sixteen. 'I normally played in midfield or on the wing, but Terry soon decided he wanted me up front,' added Glyn, who made 130 appearances (16 goals) for The Tykes. He also had a short loan spell at Doncaster Rovers before moving to the south west to join Bristol City.

For the next three seasons Glyn was virtually an ever-present, topping the scoring charts in his first two seasons, helping the club to promotion out of the Fourth Division at the end of the 1983/84 season and, two years later, playing a major role with two goals for City in their Freight Rover final success at Wembley.

'Promotion and then two trips to Wembley was a fantastic experience and great for the club and the fans, after the bad times they suffered,' said Glyn. Although City were to lose to Mansfield in the Freight Rover final the year after winning it, it was Glyn who scored in the 1–1 draw before the club lost in a penalty shoot-out.

Twice voted City's 'Player of the Year,' he shared his joy at scoring with the City fans by rushing over to the barriers to celebrate, something the supporters loved, but which brought plenty of finger-wagging from match officials. And with a total of 77 goals during his time at Ashton, there was a lot of celebrating.

It was while recovering from injury that Glyn had a short loan spell at Torquay United and was a member of the team that beat Spurs, Ray Clemence, Ossie Ardilles and all, 1–0 in a League Cup match at Plainmoor.

After nearly 250 games for City, Glyn moved on to Aldershot, where he scored five goals in 58 appearances. 'The trouble with Aldershot was that they were paying good wages, but had small crowds and eventually the club went under,' he explained.

After leaving Aldershot, Glyn was persuaded to turn out for Bath City for a short period, but a knee operation cut short his playing days. For fourteen years he went into the family curtain business, but these days he runs his own soccer schools. 'I get tremendous enjoyment from helping the youngsters,' he said.

Glyn is married with two daughters – Candace and Christine – and lives in Weston-super-Mare with his wife Machell.

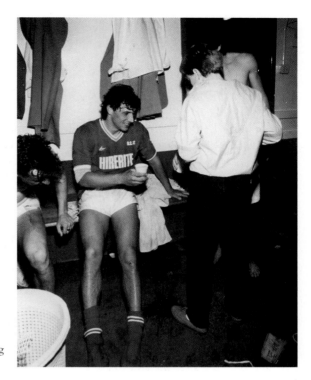

A well earned cuppa for Glyn, after helping
City clinch promotion.

Glyn Riley today.

TOM RITCHIE

'More fat on a chip' was an expression once used to describe Tom Ritchie when he first arrived at Ashton Gate. But, by the time he left the club, he had proved to be worth his weight in gold.

When a teenager, Tom made the long journey south from his native Scotland with his brother Steve, he couldn't, in his wildest dreams, have imagined what an important part he'd have to play in the history of Bristol City, achieving legendary status after close on 500 games for The Robins.

There were many at Ashton Gate who thought that younger brother Steve was the more likely of the two to make the grade, while others were more concerned that Tom was a bit too much 'on the wiry side' to withstand the rigors of professional football.

As it turned out, Steve was to make just one senior appearance, before heading back home to try his luck with Morton, while Tom was to make his mark in City's red and white. He made his senior debut in August 1972 against Millwall and got the first of his 115 Bristol City goals in a 3-3 draw with Preston, just before Christmas. He finished that season with 24 starts and by the end of the following season had firmly established himself in the side, missing just three games.

By the end of the 1974/75 season, City finished sixth in the Second Division, with the promise of better things to come. They didn't have long to wait – one season, as the club celebrated their best season in living memory with promotion to the top flight. 'Yes, that was something special,' said Tom, top scorer that year with 18 goals.

The loss of Cheesley to injury in only their second game of the new season, plus the class opposition that City faced every week, meant that it was always going to be a fight for survival, but survive they did. The following season they were still there and won the Anglo-Scottish Cup. In their third season they finished a creditable thirteenth, but the fourth year at the top saw them relegated, despite top scorer Tom's 13 goals. And so began the club's infamous slide towards the Fourth Division and financial disaster.

In 1981, with the club's overdraft rocketing by the day, City accepted an £180,000 bid for Tom from Sunderland. 'I had eighteen months there, but it didn't go well for me,' he said

Tom played 35 games for the Roker Park side, as well as 15 games on loan at Carlisle. He was put out of his north east nightmare eighteen months later, with an SOS to return 'home' to City, now languishing in the Fourth Division.

Back in Bristol, Tom became part of the restructured City side and helped The Robins gain promotion to Division Three. He went on to play for the first half of the 1984/85 season, before dropping out of the League for three years with then non-League Yeovil Town.

These days Tom, like many of his former teammates, is a postman. He lives in Portishead with his wife Doreen. They have two children, Robert and Shannon.

Right: Tom in his City days.

Below: Back for a return trip to Ashton Gate.

DAVID RODGERS

As John Lennon once said, 'Life is what happens to you while you're busy making other plans.' And that was so true for former Bristol City star David Rodgers. Having followed in his father's footsteps and signed professional forms for the club in the late 1960s, he went on to become a stalwart in the heart of the City defence, notching up over 200 senior games. Then came the crash, as the club went on to freefall out of the old First Division and lurched towards financial suicide. As is well documented, they stayed in existence only because eight senior players agreed to tear up their contracts and walk away from the club – and David was one of those eight.

'It was a very difficult time for all of us and it took a while to adapt after what happened,' he said. After leaving Ashton Gate, David had short spells with Lincoln City and Torquay United, and then spent a year in the Southern League with Forest Green Rovers, before hanging up his boots. Well actually, he never did totally hang up those boots, having taken a slight change of direction by going to work as groundsman at Bristol Grammar School. 'The school was literally at the bottom of the garden at the house where we lived, so there wasn't much travelling involved!' he said. In 1985 David 'transferred' to Bristol's Clifton College, where he coached a variety of sports including rugby, cricket and, of course, football.

But back to those City days. David's father Arnold was a bustling centre forward who had joined City from Huddersfield Town in 1949. He went on to score 111 goals for the Robins in 204 senior games before leaving City in 1956 to finish his League career at Shrewsbury Town. Rodgers junior actually beat his dad's appearance total by 16 games, 19 if you count substitute appearances. Not that, as a centre half, there was ever any danger of him passing dad's goals total. He did weigh in with 18 though.

At one stage David had thought about the possibility of going into football management, but at the time he was thinking in terms of when his playing career was over. And he certainly wasn't prepared for the premature end that City's financial plight had brought about. 'I really don't know how today's managers cope,' he said. 'They are under great pressure to get results and in most cases given very little time to do so.'

David lives in Redland with his wife, Sue. They have two daughters, Samantha who lives in London and Melanie who is in Bristol. Still at Clifton College, David is a tutor, assistant housemaster and master in charge of football to the youngsters there. And those boots that he thought he'd hung up still get an airing when he's out on the playing fields, passing on the benefit of his skills and knowledge to a younger generation.

David Rodgers in his playing days (photograph courtesy of Mike Jay).

David today at Clifton College.

LEE ROGERS

Near post or far post? It's all the same these days for former City defender Lee Rogers. For Lee, like many former City players, is a communications supplier – postman! – the number one choice of 'Civvy Street' jobs amongst the ex-pros. 'I've been "on the post" for about ten years now,' said Lee, who is based at Royal Mail's delivery office in Avonmouth.

Back in the 1980s, the only deliveries that Lee was thinking about were those being sent in by opposing footballers, while letter boxes have now taken the place of penalty boxes. 'I joined City as an apprentice in 1983 and made my debut against Wigan in the first game of the 1984/85 season,' recalled Lee. Initially under the watchful eye of manager Terry Cooper and his assistant Clive Middlemass, and later Joe Jordan, Lee made 36 senior appearances for The Robins, and was a member of the squad that won promotion to the Third Division.

Lee was also at Wembley when the City beat Bolton to win the Freight Rover Cup. 'I was injured at the time, but it was still a fantastic experience and great for the club and the fans after all the bad times they had experienced,' he said.

In the summer of 1988 Lee left the City, linking up again with former manager Terry Cooper at Exeter, where he enjoyed five happy years. It was at Exeter that Lee enjoyed one of his best moments in football. 'Our captain Shaun Taylor was injured and the boss made me skipper for the game in which we clinched promotion, which is a lovely memory,' he said with a smile. In fact, The Grecians went on to win the Fourth Division championship.

A knee operation curtailed Lee's playing days at Exeter and he moved on to Gloucester City in the Southern League. 'Brian Godfrey was the manager there and we just missed promotion to the Conference, but then the club hit financial problems and that was the end of that,' he revealed.

Next stop for Lee was Weston-super-Mare FC, where he linked up with former City striker Ricky Chandler and the much-travelled Dave Payne. 'Every club's got a joker and "Payney" was theirs. A great player, but you had to watch out for him playing a practical joke on you,' he revealed.

After eight enjoyable years at the seaside club, Lee had to put away his boots after suffering a broken leg. 'I was thirty-four and after years of playing soccer and carrying a few injuries, that last fracture spelt the end,' he admitted with a sigh.

Married to Linda, the couple live in Shirehampton and have a teenage daughter and two sons. And while Norman Hunter may have 'bitten a few legs' on the football pitch, Lee's now more concerned about family pets doing the same thing when he walks up their driveways!

Right: Lee as a young Bristol City player.

Below: Lee today at Royal Mail's Avonmouth Delivery Office.

ALFIE ROWLES

It's around sixty-seven years ago that Alfie Rowles last pulled on a Bristol City shirt. The sixteenth of September 1939 in fact.

Born in Bristol in 1916, Alfie was a natural goalscorer. His goalscoring ability first showed itself when he played in the old Bristol & District League. He moved on to finding the net on a regular basis in the Somerset League for Weston-super-Mare, before he came to the attention of a City scout, who soon had him down at Ashton Gate for a trial. And so Alfie became a professional footballer:

> In those days centre halves were tough, they really man-marked you. In fact, if you went to the loo at half-time, you half expected to find the opposing centre half stood behind you!

Come January 1938, Alfie was called up to the first team and promptly scored a hat-trick. He went on to complete the season with 18 goals from just 14 starts, setting up a new Football League record by scoring in six consecutive games, including a hat-trick of hat-tricks. 'Mind you, you didn't get to keep the match ball for a hat-trick in those days,' he said.

The footballing world was at Alfie's feet and there was even talk of a £1,000 transfer to Major Buckley's Wolverhampton Wanderers as the new season dawned. City started the new campaign well. A draw at Watford was followed by wins over Aldershot and Port Vale, with Alfie weighing in with a brace in the 5-1 victory over Port Vale.

Next on the agenda was a home game with Notts County and, with it, disaster for Alfie. 'I collided with the County keeper and was carried off with badly damaged ligaments,' he recalled. 'It was just one of those things and I certainly don't put any blame on the goalie.'

A determined man, Alfie fought hard to regain fitness, but his comeback attempts, the last being against Bristol Rovers in mid-September, confirmed what he'd already guessed – the end of the road as a professional footballer. 'It was a blow, but you just have to get on with life,' he said philosophically.

After football, Alfie went to work for Brecknell, Dolman & Rodgers. 'I was glad of the job, but it was a bit of a shock doing a twelve-hour shift after having so much spare time as a professional footballer,' he admitted. When Brecknell, Dolman & Rodgers closed down, Alfie worked as a fitter for Godwin & Warren and also had a spell with W.D. & H.O. Wills, before retiring.

A widower, Alfie often reflects on his short-lived soccer career. 'I've got some lovely memories,' he summed up. 'Sometimes I sit here at home in the evenings and think to myself, I didn't do so bad.'

Above: Alfie Rowles in action against Clapton Orient in 1938.

Right: Alfie at eighty-nine.

DAVID SEAL

Signed from the Belgian side Eendracht, Aalst in 1994, Australian David Seal featured in over sixty games for City. But, when he arrived in the UK, he was originally due to sign for West Ham. 'My agent had arranged for me to have a two-week trial with The Hammers and it was all going very well,' explained David. 'Then, on the day I was supposed to sign for them, the manager (Billy Bonds) walked out and the whole deal collapsed.'

Luckily, a trial was set up with Russell Osman's Bristol City and after just two reserve games, in which David scored six goals, he was signed up.

During his three years with City, David became a firm fans' favourite, rattling in over 30 goals. 'I loved the supporters at Ashton Gate, they always gave me a great reception which, when you're a striker, does your confidence the world of good,' he said. He also had an unexpected bonus coming to Bristol, meeting his future wife Teressa.

A change of manager saw David on his way from Ashton and off to Northampton Town. 'I'd had a couple of injuries at City, there was a change of manager and Northampton made me an offer I simply couldn't refuse, especially as our eldest daughter had just been born and we were looking for a bit more security,' explained David. But the move was not without more than a little controversy. 'Because of my injury, I initially went to Northampton on loan so that they could assess my fitness,' he pointed out 'During that time we played against City and I scored in a 2-1 win for The Cobblers. After that, most clubs had a clause written into loan deals that meant you couldn't play against your original club,' he revealed.

David enjoyed two seasons with Northampton, finishing as top scorer with 26 goals the first year and playing in the play-off final against Grimsby, losing to the opposition to just miss out on promotion.

Despite offers to stay in England – Oldham and Plymouth were among the clubs interested in signing him – David returned home to Australia to play in their national league. He returned to England and elected to leave full-time football, signing for Southern League Mangotsfield United, where he enjoyed goalscoring success – over 150 goals for the club – before leaving them last summer for Yate Town. He has subsequently re-signed for Mangotsfield.

Away from the soccer field, David is a delivery driver for a large Bristol-based food company and, at the time of writing, he was looking to become a personal fitness trainer. He lives in the Emmersons Green area of Bristol with Teressa and their two young daughters, Ellie and Jessica.

Above: Goalscoring celebrations from David Seal. (Photograph courtesy of Peter Norton Photography Ltd of Northampton)

Right: Ready for the road – David Seal today.

MARK SHAIL

Former City captain Mark Shail arrived at Ashton Gate in 1993. He came via Yeovil, Worcester and Sweden. 'My parents came from Sheffield, but dad's job took him to Sweden, which was where I was born in 1966,' explained Mark, who now lives in Flax Bourton.

Mark was born in Sandviken but his stay in Sweden lasted for just the first three years of his life, before the family returned to the UK. 'I started my playing career for Worcester City in the old Beezer Homes League, when I was seventeen,' continued Mark. It wasn't long before his displays at the heart of the Worcester defence started to attract scouts and, after four years with the club, he moved on to Yeovil Town. 'Yeovil weren't in the Football League in those days, but they were the cream of non-League football, with their famous sloping pitch and great FA Cup tradition – a wonderful family club,' he pointed out.

When experienced defender Russell Osman took over the hot seat at Bristol City, one of his priorities was to bring in a dominant centre half and City paid out £70,000 in 1993 to bring Mark to Ashton Gate. By the end of the 1993/94 season Mark was virtually an ever-present in the side, featuring in 53 senior League and cup games:

> We had a pretty decent side, finishing in mid-table in the First Division (now the Championship) and beating Liverpool at Anfield in the cup. Brian Tinnion, who signed for City at the same time as me, got the only goal of the game and it was probably the highlight of my time with the club, especially as I'd been given the captain's armband. I played under a few managers during my time at Ashton. Obviously I owe a lot to Russell Osman for the faith he showed in me, John Ward was a great motivator and Joe Jordan was a strict disciplinarian.

After seven years and over 200 games for City, Mark was on his travels, joining Kidderminster Harriers who, managed by Jan Molby, had just got into the Football League. 'I had two years there, but was always conscious that my playing career was nearing its end, so I attended the City of Bristol College to study journalism,' explained Mark. He has completed his degree, become a graduate at Surrey University, has worked for press and radio, and is now a journalist for the PFA.

Right: Mark (second left) celebrates with Andy Llewellyn, following their cup success at Liverpool.

Below: Mark Shail today, working for the PFA.

JOHN SHAW

'It was never dull,' summed up former City goalie John Shaw, as he looked back on the ups and downs between the posts at Bristol City. In the eleven years he was there, he was in and out of the side, experienced the joys of promotion and the despair of relegation and then looked on anxiously as the club nearly went bankrupt and eight of his colleagues tore up their contracts to save Bristol City from financial extinction.

Born in Stirling in 1954, John was spotted playing for a local boys club by a scout from the then mighty Leeds United. Well served by goalkeepers at Elland Road, John moved to City on a free transfer in 1976, where again he had to bide his time to dislodge resident keeper Ray Cashley. When he got his big chance he went on to make the position his own as the club enjoyed a place in the top flight. A fearless goalkeeper who commanded his penalty area, there was even talk of a call-up for Scotland.

Then it all went pear-shaped. City started their downward fall, Swedish goalie Jan Moller was brought in and John was back on the sidelines. Now the club was not only in freefall, arriving ultimately in the old Fourth Division, but more seriously, their financial situation threatened their very existence.

Jan Moller departed for no other reason than to reduce the club's astronomical wage bill, and shortly afterwards eight first-team regulars – the 'Ashton Gate Eight' – were 'out of work'. Wasn't he concerned that he'd be one of them? 'Not really,' he replied. 'Whatever they did with the playing staff, they had to have a goalkeeper!'

And so it was that John reclaimed his place in the first XI and became one of the stalwarts who were determined to play their part in getting City back up the divisions. And to the delight of a full house at Ashton, the team, with John between the sticks, clinched promotion to the Third Division by beating local rivals Swindon in their last home game.

In 1985, after eleven turbulent years at Bristol City, it was time for John to move on – down the motorway to Exeter City, where he enjoyed another two years of League action, before stepping down to non-League football with Gloucester City. He was to enjoy two more seasons as custodian, before calling it a day.

Conscious that a footballer's career is a short one, John had already turned his hand to painting and decorating, having been encouraged by teammate Forbes Phillipson-Masters, who had gone down the same road. These days he is just as professional as a painter and decorator as he was in commanding his penalty area in those not-so-dull days at Bristol City.

Paul and his wife Jean, who is a civilian worker at the local police headquarters, live in Portishead.

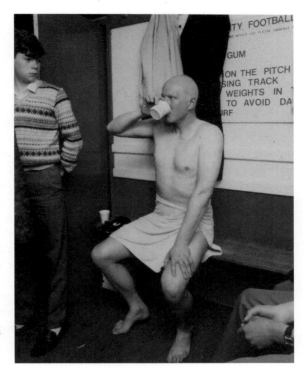

1984, and keeper John Shaw enjoys a cuppa after helping City to win promotion from the Fourth Division.

Brushing up on his painting skills.

ALAN SKIRTON

Six months' National Service in the Army Pay Corp was obviously not time wasted for former Bristol City winger Alan Skirton, for after hanging up his boots, he was to work miracles as commercial manager at Bath City and then Yeovil Town. Not that he would have needed too much financial acumen to handle his first wage packet as a professional footballer – £1 a week!

Born in Bath, Alan joined Arsenal in 1960, having been rejected as a teenage amateur by City. 'My first weekly wage at Highbury was the princely sum of a pound a week,' said Alan. But Alan's career as a pro footballer was very nearly over before it had begun.

'I'd only played a couple of reserve games when I contracted TB. I was in hospital for four-and-a-half months and out of the game for a year-and-a-half,' he recalled. 'Arsenal were absolutely marvellous.' Alan went on to enjoy 144 games in The Gunners' first team, netting 53 goals in the process. 'There were some quality players there,' he said with a smile. 'George Eastham, Joe Baker, Georgie Armstrong... quality players.'

The 1966/67 season saw Alan leave Highbury's famous marbled halls and move to the seaside to play for Blackpool, where he played 77 League games, scoring 29 goals, including one at Highbury.

The chance to return to the West Country was too good to turn down, so when City put in a bid of £15,000 he headed home:

> That was in November 1968 and City were struggling at the wrong end of the Second Division, but they did have a great strike pair up front of Chris Garland and John Galley. I was brought in to supply the ammunition for them, as well as to get a few goals myself.

Alan found the back of the net 18 times for The Robins in his 90-plus appearances in City's red and white, with many fans remembering the goal he got in a 1-1 draw with Spurs in the first leg of the League Cup semi-final at Ashton Gate.

At the end of the 1970/71 season Alan, now thirty-two years old, was released to join Torquay United, where he put in 38 senior appearances, netting seven times. 'After that I had five months playing for Durban City in South Africa,' he said.

Returning home, Alan saw out his playing days with Weymouth and Bath City, taking on the role of commercial manager at Twerton Park. 'I had nine years of that and turned the fundraising side of the club around.'

Despite his success, Alan found himself looking for a new position – a wait of just one week. 'Yeovil Town offered me the commercial manager's job with them and I took it. Mind you, I had no idea how badly off the club was, they really were in financial intensive care.' Taking to his task like a duck to water, Alan went on to raise over £450,000 for the club, before stepping down after twenty-one years of much-appreciated service. 'I am so glad the club are doing so well,' he said. 'They made me a life member and I often go to watch them play.'

Like many of his former teammates, Alan has had hip replacement surgery. Married to Jane, the couple live in Bradford-on-Avon. 'I'd like to think that every club I've been at has got its money's worth,' summed up Alan – and at £1 a week, none more so than Arsenal!

Above: Alan (far left, second row from the top) in his Arsenal days.

Right: Quids-in – Alan's first wage and contract.

PAUL STEVENS

When promising right-back Paul Stevens signed on as an apprentice for Bristol City in 1976, they'd just won promotion to the top flight. By the time he was in his sixth season at the club they were bottom of the Fourth Division! Not that you could lay the blame for this disastrous fall at Paul's door. 'I made my debut just after my eighteenth birthday at Middlesbrough and didn't get back in the first team for three years!' he pointed out.

The eighth of April 1978 was the date that Paul made his first senior start. 'That's probably one of my best footballing memories,' recalled Paul. 'Putting on the shirt and knowing that I'd got a first-team game – a wonderful experience.'

Although City lost the game at Ayresome Park 2-0, Paul had a sound match, but the following week Gerry Sweeney was back from suspension to reclaim his place in the side. 'Gerry and Donnie Gillies, both good players, were ahead of me in the pecking order for the right-back spot, so I just had to be patient and wait for my chance to come again,' Paul explained.

The departure of Gillies to neighbours Rovers in the summer of 1980 offered Paul the chance to push for a place, although Sweeney wore the no.2 shirt right through the first half of the season, until switching positions to give Paul an end-of-season run of 15 games.

'The club had gone down to the old Second Division and Bob Houghton had taken over from Alan Dicks and he kept me in the side,' said Paul. Sadly, the club was very much on a downward spiral which culminated in relegation.

An ever-present the following season, the club continued to freefall down the League, the 'Ashton Gate Eight' having departed, leaving the club without their most experienced players. Now under the management of Terry Cooper – Bob Houghton and Roy Hodgson had both come and gone from the managerial hot seat – the club found themselves in the basement division. 'At one time we were bottom of the Fourth, and you can't get much lower than that,' admitted Paul.

Gradually, Cooper steadied the sinking ship and the club finished in mid-table, although Paul played just 15 times that term. The following year, though, he was an ever-present as Cooper restored some pride in the team by guiding them to promotion. 'That was a great experience after we had struggled for so long,' said Paul. 'Clinching promotion at Chester was fantastic and our fans were superb.'

Back in the Third Division, Paul made 37 senior starts, as the club just missed out on another promotion season, finishing in fifth position. Released by City in 1985, Paul had five years with Bath City, but suffering with persistent knee problems, he gave up playing in 1990. 'It just catches up with you in the end and I went four years without even kicking a ball,' he told me.

Away from the professional spotlight, Paul moved into selling. These days he's the UK sales manager for sports equipment company Mizuno, overseeing the company's UK sales force and key accounts.

Home for Paul is in Ashton, just a back pass away from the City ground. He is married to Joanne and they have a daughter Mollie, who plays in the Bristol City Girls Academy. Paul also has a son, Danny, and daughter, Kelly, from his first marriage.

Above: Celebrating promotion, Paul (arms raised) acknowledges the fans.

Right: Off on his travels for Mizuno, Paul Stevens today.

CON SULLIVAN

From the Downs League to the marbled halls of Highbury, via Bristol City, that's Con Sullivan's rags-to-riches story.

Now in his late seventies, Con's soccer story began in earnest when he was spotted playing Downs League football for Horfield Old Boys. Bristol City manager Bob Wright followed up the advice of his scouts and signed the then twenty-one-year-old goalkeeper. Playing in the old Third Division (South), Con lined up with the likes of Don Clark, Ivor Guy, Den Roberts and Ernie Peacock. 'And don't forget Alec Eisentrager,' said Con. 'People go on about foreign players in today's game, but we had our overseas import in little Alec – a very good player – from Germany via a POW camp.'

By the end of the 1952/53 season, Con had established himself in the City goal and was an ever-present that season. But his skill and bravery 'between the sticks' had not gone unnoticed by 'the big boys' and, in February 1954, after 78 senior games for The Robins, he was off to the bright lights of London and the hallowed Highbury halls, for an undisclosed fee:

A totally different world. There were over eighty players on their books and eight of them were goalkeepers. The funny thing was I'd never even been to London until I signed for The Gunners!

Not that the move to one of English football's giants meant a hefty wage increase, even if you were playing to crowds of 65,000:

You have to remember that those were the days of the maximum wage. I was on twelve quid a week in the season and a tenner during the summer. There were some great players around then: Nat Lofthouse, Trevor Ford, John Charles – the best of them – and my old mate Derek Tapscott. I was best man at his wedding and we met up recently at a surprise party to mark his golden wedding anniversary.

Sadly, Con's Highbury adventure of over 100 senior games came to a premature end. Bravely diving at the feet of a Birmingham City centre forward, Con took a hefty kick in the shoulder. 'It was a fifty–fifty ball there to be won and I don't blame the lad who kicked me,' said Con.

With his soccer career over, Con worked for many years as a forklift driver, before retiring in 1992. Over the years, the physical effects of playing soccer in the 1950s had caught up with him and he's had operations to his shoulder, hips and knee. If that wasn't enough, he's also undergone treatment for cancer of the colon. 'All of which means I can't even play skittles anymore – but I'm a dab hand at crib!'

Right: In action for Arsenal.

Below: An ace goalkeeper, it's crib for Con now.

GERRY SWEENEY

For a man who 'stamped' his personality on the game at Ashton Gate, it was perhaps ironic that former City captain Gerry Sweeney would continue making first-class deliveries – not the long ball passing kind, but ones in envelopes. For after playing League football until thirty-seven years of age, Gerry, like many of his former colleagues, became a postman.

Born in Glasgow in 1945, Gerry joined The Robins in the summer of 1971 as a winger from Morton. Prior to joining City, Gerry played in three Scottish semi-finals and one final on Hampden Park's hallowed turf. 'Hampden Park is a bit special and, although we lost, it was an honour to play there,' summed up the likeable Scot.

Gerry began his City career in midfield but, although there were a few raised eyebrows when manager Alan Dicks moved him to right-back, Gerry proved the doubters wrong with consistent performances. His strengths – his superb fitness that could leave a younger player standing in his slipstream, his ability to read the game and his composure under pressure – were to stand him in good stead as the club climbed to the dizzy heights of the First Division. He was also, for some time, the club's penalty taker, but his penalty taking style – practically a one step back and shoot man – had many supporters with their hearts in their mouths.

Having enjoyed the good times and the rise to the dizzy heights of the top division, Gerry then suffered the ignominy of relegation after just a few seasons at the top, with Bristol City plummeting down the divisions. As if that wasn't bad enough, Gerry was one of those players who agreed to tear up their contracts when the club faced bankruptcy.

For a servant that deserved more, Gerry was to finish his League career at lowly York City. When his playing days were over he was appointed assistant manager at Walsall, getting a great reception from the Ashton Gate crowd when he made a point of running to the four corners of the pitch to applaud his former supporters, prior to his Walsall team taking the field.

When Gerry left pro soccer he took on the role of postman. But there was still one chapter to come in the football career of Gerry Sweeney. A certain Joe Jordan took over the Ashton Gate 'hot seat' and promptly offered Gerry a position as his number two. Gerry jumped at the offer, but sadly the fickle fate of soccer management did its usual heartless trick and Jordan was sacked. Mind you, when Jordan was dismissed, Gerry became City's most successful manager, albeit in a caretaker role, playing one and winning one, before making way for the new management team.

Fortunately for Gerry, Royal Mail were more than happy to take him back on their books and these days he's a familiar sight on the streets of Portishead, still making those first-class deliveries.

Gerry during his City days.

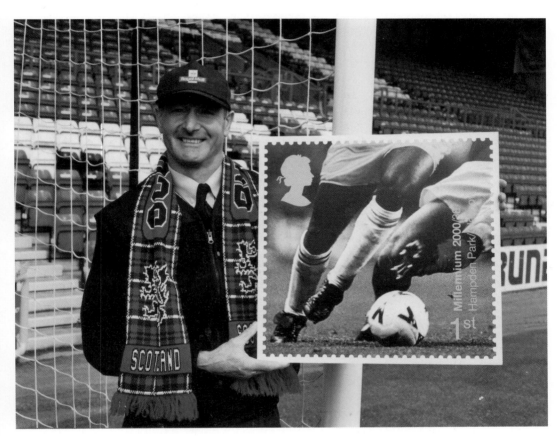

Back on the Ashton Gate pitch, this time for a Royal Mail stamp promotion.

TREVOR TAINTON

There's an old saying: 'the quiet ones are always the worst.' But in football, the reverse is often the case. The unsung hero who quietly and methodically gets on with his job, without taking all the plaudits or forever grabbing the headlines. Such a man was Trevor Tainton.

Usually to be found wearing the no.7 shirt – years before silly squad numbers came along – Trevor could best be described as City's workhorse in the midfield department. He made his debut in a home victory against Carlisle in September 1967, but, with the departure of manager Fred Ford just around the corner, he made only another three starts that season. The following year he was limited to a handful of starts, but the season after he established himself in the squad, with over thirty appearances.

By the end of the 1971/72 season Trevor was a first-team regular. An unsung hero he may have been, but his quiet midfield efficiency hadn't gone unnoticed. Liverpool's legendary manager Bill Shankly had a £50,000 offer knocked back, as Alan Dicks set about building a side capable of promotion to the First Division. In 1976 the dream came true, as City made it to the top flight, with Trevor an ever-present in that historic promotion season.

Wonderful times for everyone at Bristol City, with four years in the First Division. Then, after the highs, came the lows, as City were relegated in two successive seasons. Even worse, the club's very existence was threatened, as their ever-increasing overdraft was causing more concern than their footballing problems.

Trevor made the last of his 556 starts on 30 January 1981 in a 1-1 draw at Newport County. Then, along with seven of his teammates, he agreed to tear up his contract and walk away from Ashton, in order to ensure the club's very existence. 'Those were very difficult times for us,' said Trevor. 'Most of us had commitments – families, mortgages and so on – it was very hard.'

Finishing his League career at Torquay United, where he played 19 games, Trevor left League football to play in the Southern League with Trowbridge and Forest Green.

Including substitute appearances, Trevor was just 11 games short of 600 appearances for The Robins in over fourteen seasons – only City legend John Atyeo had played more games for the club. Never a prolific goalscorer, Trevor found the net 30 times for the team.

These days Trevor is a security guard/shift leader at the British Nuclear Power Station in Oldbury. He lives with his partner Glenda and has two grown-up sons. 'I must be getting old – I'm a grandfather now,' he said with a smile. 'I do a lot of shift work, so don't get down to the ground very often, but I will always be a City fan. I've got some wonderful memories and no one can take that away from me.'

Trevor in City's colours.

Trevor on duty at the power station.

BRIAN TINNION

On paper it was 'a marriage made in heaven'. Brian Tinnion, the man who had succeeded Danny Wilson as manager and who had got Bristol City to within one point of the play-offs in his first season in charge, was expected to lead City to automatic promotion the following year.

'Tinman', as he was nicknamed by many supporters, was a firm fans' favourite on the pitch, having notched up over 500 appearances for The Robins. A number of (on paper) match-winning signings seemed to endorse all the pundits' predictions that his City team would finish in the top two, probably as champions. But, as we all know in the cruel and fickle world of soccer, the only certainty is that nothing is certain, other than the fact that soccer has a nasty habit of kicking you in the teeth.

'We so much wanted it to work,' said Brian. A bad start to the season, culminating in a disastrous 7-1 defeat at Swansea, spelt the end of what, until that fateful season, had been a happy time for Brian at City.

It was in 1993 that Brian arrived at Ashton Gate, with Russell Osman signing the cultured midfield player for £150,000 from Bradford City. Born in County Durham, Brian began his career with Newcastle United and was a member of their youth team that won the FA Youth Cup in 1985. One of his teammates from that young Geordie side was a certain Paul Gascoigne.

Brian was to make a mere 32 appearances for The Magpies, mainly at left-back, before he moved to Bradford City for a £180,000 transfer fee in March 1989. Bradford's management team had realised that midfield was the best place for Brian's cultured left foot and he went on to make 145 appearances for The Bantams, before coming to the south west. And, of course, Brian's status as a cult hero was guaranteed when he scored City's winner in that memorable cup success at Anfield.

'I settled in quite quickly at City and getting a goal in one of my first games didn't do me any harm,' said Brian, with a smile. And the goal at Liverpool? 'Now that was a goal I'm never going to forget,' was his response.

A bout of glandular fever halted Brian's progress during Joe Jordan's managerial reign, but the arrival of John Ward (and later Danny Wilson) saw Brian come into his own. A member of the side that lost in the Auto Windscreens final at Wembley in 2000, Brian was in the City line-up that took the trophy (although renamed the LDV Vans Trophy), when they beat Carlisle United at The Millennium Stadium three years later.

At the end of the 2003/04 season, City returned to Cardiff for the Division One play-off final with Brighton. As we all know, City played nowhere near their best, losing 1-0, a result that was to see the departure of Danny Wilson and the step up to manager for Brian.

And that's where we came in. A certainty in most peoples' eyes to be in a City all-time greats line-up (certainly in mine) Brian made 497 full appearances, plus 54 as sub, during his twelve years at City, scoring 42 goals, many of them match-winning penalties.

After leaving City, Brian put on his playing boots again and had a short spell in the Conference with Aldershot Town. But, when one door shuts another one opens and the chance of taking up a new challenge, with a move to Southern Spain as part of Charlton Athletic's youth development scheme there, was tailor made for the talented Geordie. 'My wife Katherine and I have wanted to move out there and I am looking forward to the new challenge,' said Brian, shortly before his departure in July.

Left: Brian in his City days.

Below: Bound for Spain, Brian Tinnion and young son Jay.

ALAN WALSH

'My five years at City were the best of my career, although I would dearly have loved to have hit the magic 100,' said Alan Walsh, who, at the end of his time at Ashton Gate, had netted 99 goals. 'Sometimes you remember the shots that hit the woodwork and you think if just one of those had gone in…'

Born in County Durham, Alan began his football career with nearby Middlesbrough in 1977. He was to make just three senior appearances for Boro, before joining Darlington and establishing himself as a natural goalscorer, with a deadly left foot.

Between 1978 and 1984 Alan played over 250 games for The Quakers, finding the back of the net over 100 times, with most of his goals being his trademark blockbusters, or should that be net busters? Very soon he was attracting the scouts to The Feethams, but Darlington had every right to feel hard done to when a Football League tribunal decided that £18,000 would be the price City would have to pay to bring him to Ashton Gate. Certainly the biggest heist since The Great Train Robbery!

'In my first season at City we just missed promotion. Later we went on to play two successive Freight Rover finals at Wembley, lost out to Walsall over a three-match play-off marathon and reached the semi-finals of the Littlewoods Cup,' recalled Alan, who finished the 1987/88 season as top scorer with 15 goals and was voted Player of the Year.

Just one goal short of the '100 Club', Alan left City in 1989 for Besiktas in Turkey, where he helped his new team win the League and cup. 'That was an unforgettable experience playing over there,' he said. 'Obviously it's a totally different culture, but they were very football orientated.'

After returning home Alan had four-and-a-half years as Football Community Officer with arch rivals Rovers. 'After so long at City it felt a little odd at first, but they all made me very welcome,' he said.

Alan 'came home' to City in 2000, taking on a coaching role looking after the Under-17s and Under-19s, before a restructuring saw him become Development Coach, working with the youngsters and the senior players. 'The future's looking good at City,' he pointed out. 'A number of very good players have progressed through the Academy to the first team and in these days that's vital for the future of the club.'

Married to Sue, the couple live in Portishead and have four children – Stuart, Kayte, Sophie and Phillip.

There have been a few ups and downs here in recent years, but people talk about Bristol City as a sleeping giant – and it is. With the right mix of young talent and experienced players, the future looks very bright.

Above: Alan (back row, second from the left) in a pre-match line-up.

Right: A penny for his thoughts, as Alan reflects on life at Ashton Gate.

JOHNNY WATKINS

Bowling along nicely, that's former Bristol City star Johnny Watkins, who gets as much pleasure playing bowls as he did tearing down the wing at Ashton Gate. 'A few of the old boys took the game up after they finished playing football and I've been playing bowls now for well over twenty years and love it.'

Back in the 1950s and early '60s, it was footballs not bowling bowls that Johnny was interested in. Spotted playing for local Bristol side Clifton St Vincents, he signed professional forms for City in 1953. Between then and 1959, he notched up more than a century of senior appearances in City's first team, scoring 21 goals in the process. Many of these came from the penalty spot, as he assumed the mantle of spot-kick king for The Robins, going on to score 14 consecutive successful penalties during his career.

A firm crowd favourite, his skills up front attracted the attention of Cardiff City and in 1959 he crossed over the border to Wales to delight the fans at Ninian Park. 'In my first season for Cardiff we won promotion to the First Division and regularly attracted home gates of more than 35,000,' he said. A major factor in Cardiff's rise to the football elite that season was Johnny's contribution of 18 goals.

In 1961 Johnny returned to Bristol, signing for Bert Tann's Bristol Rovers side. A one-and-a-half year spell with The Pirates saw a return of 40 games and three goals.

'After Rovers I had the chance to stay in the League,' he pointed out. 'Plymouth Argyle were interested, as were a couple of clubs from up north, but we were settled in Bristol and didn't really want to move out of the area.' He was also conscious that he had a wife and family to keep and the financial rewards that many players enjoy today were not around. 'When I finished playing professionally, my weekly wage was between £10 and £12, rising to £20 if we qualified for win bonuses and so on.'

Dropping out of the Football League, Johnny plied his trade with Chippenham, Welton Rovers and then Bath City. He was also working in the offices of Brecknell, Dolman and Rogers and later moved on to work for twenty years in the offices of Rolls Royce.

Although Johnny was enjoying playing his football at Bath City, he was getting tired – literally – of the travelling involved. 'You have to remember that these were the pre-motorway days and we would often get back from an away match at two or three in the morning, snatch a few hours sleep and then get up to go to work,' he explained. And so he called time on his playing days.

These days, Johnny can be found at home with his wife Rita in their Coombe Dingle home. They have two children, Debra (who was born while Johnny was playing an away match at Blackpool) and Paul, plus four grandchildren.

Above: Another successful penalty kick by Johnny Watkins.

Right: Bowls is now Johnny's sporting passion.

KEITH WELCH

Ask any Bristol City supporter to nominate the best goalkeeper at the club from the past twenty years and it's a pretty fair bet that the name Keith Welch will feature quite prominently. During his eight years with The Robins, the Bolton-born custodian featured in over 300 senior games and became a firm fans' favourite, with his safe handling, confident control of his penalty area and the ability to pull off saves that would normally have beaten lesser shot-stoppers. 'I enjoyed my time at City,' reflected Keith. 'Getting promotion under John Ward and winning an FA Cup match at Liverpool are two of the memories that really stand out.'

Keith's professional football career began at Fourth Division Rochdale, managed by Vic Halom and, later, former Leeds legend Eddie Gray and Jimmy Lumsden, the latter going on to manage Bristol City. 'I made my debut at eighteen in a Freight Rover game against Chesterfield,' recalled Keith. His performances in goal for The Dale didn't go unnoticed and soon the scouts were checking out the young goalkeeper. The £200,000 cheque Rochdale received from City was enough to see him head for Bristol, where he was to link up again with Lumsden, by then City's manager.

'I played under a few managers during my time at Ashton Gate – Jimmy (Lumsden), Russell Osman, Joe Jordan, John Ward and Benny Leonardson – all very different from each other,' said Keith. That first season – 1991/92 – Keith made 28 League appearances, with another fine goalkeeper, Andy Leaning, taking the keepers' position for the other 20. The following season Keith made the no.1 position his own, missing only one game, a feat he repeated the season after that.

As we all know, nothing is forever in professional football and in 1999, Keith moved on, signing for Northampton Town, then managed by recent Bristol Rovers boss Ian Atkins. 'I enjoyed it at Northampton and stayed for three years,' said Keith.

After Northampton came spells at Tranmere, Torquay and Mansfield. It was at Tranmere though that Keith's career came to an end. 'I badly dislocated my shoulder in a freak training ground accident and though I tried to come back, it wasn't to be,' said Keith philosophically.

Like many pros who had moved to the West Country, Keith always planned to come back to the Bristol area. 'It was always my intention to return when my playing days were over, it's a lovely part of the world,' he pointed out. 'I got involved in property development – buying houses, doing them up and then selling them – and that's what I do today.' Married to Deborah, the couple have two young daughters and live a couple of hundred yards from Clevedon seafront. 'I was very lucky,' summed up Keith. 'I've played over 700 senior games and played in every division bar the Premiership.'

Right: Keith in action for Bristol City.

Below: Keith today working on another property project.

JACK WHITE

'Today's footballers? There are some brilliant ones about, but I'm afraid that there are far too many cheats for my liking.' This was former Bristol City stalwart Jack White's response, when asked about the footballers of today.

Born in Doncaster in 1924, Jack started his working life the hard way – in the coalfields of Yorkshire – before signing on for Aldershot in 1946. Like his younger brother Len, a striker who played with distinction at Newcastle United and Huddersfield Town, Jack started out as a centre forward. And what Jack lacked in height – he stood just over 5ft 8ins in his stockinged feet – he made up for with his ability to get in powerful headers, despite the attention of taller man-markers.

After six seasons at Aldershot, making over 200 appearances and scoring 24 goals, Jack signed for City for a fee of £5,300 – a sizeable fee back in 1952. City's manager, Pat Beesley, recognising Jack's leadership skills, immediately made him captain of the side.

By now playing in an attacking wing half role, Jack immediately made his presence felt on the pitch. After finishing fifth and then third in his first two seasons, Jack led the team to promotion, when they took the Third Division (South) championship at the end of the 1954/55 season, Leyton Orient finishing nine points behind them in second place.

'City had some very good players during the time that I was there,' recalled Jack. 'Left-winger Jack Boxley was an excellent crosser of the ball and 'Big' John (Atyeo) was a wonderful goalscorer.' So what about opposing players? 'Probably the best couple I've played against were England captain Johnny Haynes and Welsh wizard Ivor Allchurch,' replied Jack.

Jack went on to enjoy 227 games (and 11 goals) for The Robins, finally leaving Ashton Gate in March 1958 to test his leadership skills as a football manager. He went to non-League Cambridge City as player-manager and followed that with a couple of years as the gaffer at Telford United.

After soccer, Jack went to work for Brecknell, Dolman and Rogers as a service engineer, based in Kent. A widower, Jack lives in Essex. He has a son, two daughters, seven grandchildren and one great-grandchild.

'It was nice to be here today, watch the game and see some of the lads, but my football these days is confined to watching it on the television,' said Jack at a recent old boys' reunion. 'Some brilliant players – but far too much cheating.'

Jack (centre, front row) in a 1950s City team photo.

A more recent picture of Jack at a City old boys' reunion.

CLIVE WHITEHEAD

Skilful and fast, Clive Whitehead was one of those young wingers to truly earn the tag of 'exciting'. He can also point out that it was his goal against Portsmouth that guaranteed City promotion to the First Division. And it was his precision cross that gave Paul Cheesley the chance to score the only goal of the game in their opening fixture in the First Division at Arsenal.

Birmingham-born Clive joined City's ranks in 1973. He made a scoring debut at Millwall and went on to complete 11 starts in his first season. By the time the 1976/77 season was over, he was an ever-present on the wing.

Like many such talented players, only one thing was missing from Clive's game – consistency. One week at his match-winning brilliant best, the next he could be anonymous. And when manager Alan Dicks brought in a new left-winger – Gert Meijer – Clive's place in the side looked precarious. However, Dicks did keep Clive in the side, but astounded everyone by putting him in at left-back. The switch worked, with Clive effortlessly adjusting to his new role like the proverbial duck to water. He even demonstrated his versatility further by also performing as a central defender.

But as one of the more saleable assets and with the club in deep financial trouble, Clive agreed to tear up his lucrative long-term contract and moved to West Bromwich Albion for a £100,000 fee. He had made 254 starts for The Robins, scoring 16 goals. He went on to make 168 appearances for The Baggies during his five years with the club, had a short loan spell at Wolves and then moved to the South Coast to play for Portsmouth, where he played 65 times. Clive finished his League career with two seasons at Exeter City.

'When I finished playing I did a bit of coaching for (Bristol) City, but after two years decided I was better off out of it,' said Clive. He worked for one of the leading banks for a while, before he finally found his niche – working for the Professional Footballers Association (PFA). 'I cover London to Lands End, helping PFA members with contracts, pensions, that sort of thing,' explained Clive. 'It means helping and dealing with people that I know and I get a tremendous amount of job satisfaction from it.'

The father of twin daughters, Clive lives with his wife Heather in the beautiful village of Weir near Axbridge.

Clive (front row, third from right) in a pre-season Portsmouth team photo. (Picture courtesy of *The News*, Portsmouth)

PFA's Clive Whitehead today.

ALAN & GARY WILLIAMS

The old adage 'like father like son' is often very true. But in the case of Alan and Gary Williams it's so true it's quite spooky. Both played centre half for Bristol City; father Alan in the 1950s and early '60s, and son Gary in the late '70s and '80s. Both left City to try pastures new, but went on to play for the same two clubs after they left Bristol. Oh yes, and both became publicans at the end of their playing days.

Williams senior joined the ground staff at Ashton Gate in 1953. Regarded as one of the best young prospects to arrive at City, he even got a call-up in 1959 for the England Under-23s while doing his National Service with the RAF. Unfortunately, what should have been one of the highlights of his career was denied him when the match — versus Scotland — was cancelled due to bad weather.

Alan had made his debut for City in February 1957 in a 3-1 defeat at Blackburn Rovers. He went on to make the no. 5 shirt his own, but his form dipped when the club was relegated to the Third Division at the end of the 1959/60 season and he moved on to Oldham Athletic. He was to enjoy four seasons there, clocking up 172 appearances and scoring nine goals in the process. One of those appearances was at Ashton Gate against his old club in 1965, when City won 2-0 to get promotion to the Second Division.

After Oldham, Alan headed south to play for Watford for a further 43 Football League appearances, then on to Newport County (63 appearances) and finally Swansea Town, where his four-year spell brought him 146 starts. Back home in Bristol, Alan finished his playing days as player-manager at Keynsham Town and Almondsbury. Like many of his counterparts and former colleagues at that time, Alan became a publican.

Eight years after dad's last League appearance, it was the turn of Williams junior to follow in his father's footsteps, joining Bristol City as an apprentice. Primarily a centre half, son Gary went on to make over 100 senior appearances, before borrowing dad's roadmaps to follow his trails to Swansea and Oldham Athletic. Gary was to enjoy six years at Boundary Park, having switched to the left of midfield, where he enjoyed goalscoring success with over 20 goals. 1991 saw Gary on the road again, moving north to play for Hearts.

Gary's next move involved ditching road maps and digging out his passport, as like a lot of soccer pros reaching the end of their career, he flew off to play in Hong Kong. 'That was a great experience and a lot of former League players, such as Alan Walsh, Ralph Milne, Stevie Neville and Mike Fillery were out there playing,' explained Gary.

On his return Gary finished up his playing days at Bath City, but was conscious that it was time to look for a new career. So, having followed in Williams senior's footsteps on many an occasion, he turned to the licensed trade. 'Dad had been in the pub game for a while, so when he offered to help me get set up, the idea appealed to me,' he said.

These days father and son can often be seen together behind the bar of the Horse and Groom, just off the centre of Bristol.

Above: Centre half Alan Williams finds the net for City in a Second Division game against Middlesbrough.

Right: Twenty years on and it's son Gary in action for The Robins.

Below: Make that a double. Alan and Gary Williams behind the bar at the Horse and Groom.

BOBBY WILLIAMS

Quite a few footballers have had to hang up their boots because of injury – broken legs, cartilage problems, ligament damage – the list goes on. But Bobby 'Shadow' Williams had to pack up the game with more injuries than you could pack into a dozen episodes of *Casualty* and *Holby City*!

'I had a collapsed lung, six broken ribs, a fractured pelvis, dislocated hip, broken jaw and smashed eye socket,' said Bobby. Not that these horrific injuries were attributed to some tough-tackling defender. They were inflicted on him when he was involved in a car crash, while driving back from a match. 'I was on my way home after playing for Weymouth,' he recalled. 'One minute I was driving through fog and the next minute my car and I came off second best in an argument with a wall!'

Bobby was to spend six weeks in Basingstoke Hospital and took the best part of two years to recover, but as he says, it could have been worse.

Bobby signed for Bristol City in 1958. An old-fashioned scheming inside left, he earned the nickname 'Shadow' for his ability to ghost into goalscoring positions. He enjoyed the best spell of his career in City's red and white playing alongside 'Big' John Atyeo and Brian Clark, with his best friend Jantzen Derrick supplying the ammunition from the wing.

From 1958 until 1965, City's promotion year from the Third Division, Bobby played 214 senior games, netting 82 goals. But, after losing his place, Bobby found himself on his way out of Ashton Gate and heading for Second Division Rotherham United for a fee of just under £10,000. 'I wasn't really that keen to move, but that's the nature of the job I suppose,' he summed up. Although a reluctant mover to Millmoor, one of his best soccer memories was while wearing a Rotherham shirt, scoring a hat-trick over Cardiff City, John Charles and all.

After nearly two seasons at Rotherham, where he scored 12 goals in 47 games, the chance to return to Bristol, albeit for 'the old enemy' – Bristol Rovers – was too good to turn down and Bobby came home. 'Looking back that wasn't really a good move and Rovers really didn't work out for me,' he confessed. Twenty-nine appearances and five goals later, Shadow was on his way again, this time to Reading. 'I really enjoyed it there – in fact I still live in the area and still do some scouting for them,' he said.

After two seasons with The Royals, Bobby tried his luck overseas, spending a season playing for ASO Ostend in the Belgian Third Division.

After Belgium, Bobby played for Cheltenham Town (then still a non-League side) managed by former teammate Bobby Etheridge for a short spell, before his ill-fated move to Weymouth.

With his soccer career over, Bobby became a sales rep for a time, before going to work for an American oil company in Reading, then retiring. He and his wife Brenda live in the Tilehurst area of Reading. They have one son and three grandchildren.

Above: Bobby Williams (second left) in striking action.

Right: Finding his bearings back in Bristol, Bobby 'Shadow' Williams.

Other titles published by STADIA

Bristol City Football Club 1966-2002
TOM HOPEGOOD & DAVID WOODS

Life at Ashton Gate has never been dull, and the period covered by this book encompasses four promotions, five relegations, three Wembley appearances, cup wins over Chelsea and Liverpool, boardroom battles and numerous managerial changes. Stars like Geoff Merrick, John Galley, Gerry Sweeney and Mick Harford all feature, making this an essential volume for all City fans.
0 7524 2417 3

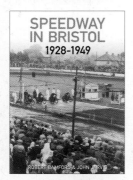

Bristol City Football Club 1894-1967
TOM HOPEGOOD

This book tells the story of Bristol City FC, from the early days of Bristol South End in the 1890s through to the mid-1960s. During this eventful period, City adopted professionalism, were elected into the Football League, finished as runners-up in the top flight of English football, reached an FA Cup final and even won the Welsh Cup! Containing a lot of rare material, this book will appeal to all fans of the club
0 7524 2040 2

Speedway in Bristol 1928-1949
ROBERT BAMFORD & JOHN JARVIS

Speedway first came to Bristol in 1928 at the Knowle Stadium. The first period of racing came to an end in 1930, but the sport returned in 1936, when the club acquired the nickname 'Bulldogs'. For a while Bristol were the best supported team in the Provincial League, also spending a season in the top division before the war. After hostilities ceased, another terrific promotion to Division One was achieved in 1949. This is the definitive history of Bristol Speedway up to that time.
0 7524 3788 7

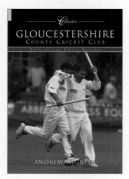

Gloucestershire CCC Classic Matches
ANDREW HIGNELL

Gloucestershire CCC has had no shortage of exciting and significant matches over the years. Since the days of the great Dr W.G. Grace, many illustrious players have graced the county grounds and entertained the crowds with their exploits. This selection aims to present the fifty most significant first-class matches in terms of the history of the county. The text is accompanied by many wonderful illustrations and a scorecard is included for each match.
0 7524 3212 5

If you are interested in purchasing other books published by Stadia, or in case you have difficulty finding any Stadia books in your local bookshop, you can also place orders directly through the Tempus Publishing website

www.tempus-publishing.com